NSCA's Strength and Conditioning Manual for High School Coaches

ISBN: 1-58518-771-2
Library of Congress Control Number: 2002116087
Book layout: Deborah Oldenburg and Jennifer Bokelmann
Diagrams: Deborah Oldenburg
Cover design: John Conner

Healthy Learning
P.O. Box 1828
Monterey, CA 93942
www.healthylearning.com

ACKNOWLEDGMENTS

The NSCA would like to thank the following individuals
for their contributions to this manual:

Dan Benardot, PhD, RD, LD
Georgia State University

Randy Best, MBA, CSCS, *D

Richard Borden, PhD, PT, CSCS
Northern Arizona University

Bruce Harbach, CSCS, *D
Wilson High School, West Lawn, PA

Ian Jeffreys, MSc, CSCS, *D
Coleg Powys: Brecon, Wales

Patrick McHenry, MA, CSCS
Ponderosa High School, Parker, CO

The NSCA would also like to thank Jess Skidmore, William Robinson,
Richard Moody, Patrick McHenry, and Ponderosa High School
for their assistance with the photographs.

CONTENTS

CHAPTER 1

Introduction

The *NSCA Strength and Conditioning Manual for High School Coaches* is designed to provide basic information to the high school strength and conditioning coach. This book includes basic information, exercise descriptions, sample programs, and a section on teaching resistance training in a high-school, classroom setting. It is designed to supplement proper education, training, and other quality educational resources.

Benefits of a Resistance Training Program

Resistance training can provide many benefits, depending on how the program is designed. With lower resistance and higher repetitions, muscular endurance can be increased. High resistance and low repetitions will help to improve muscular strength. To produce benefits, the muscles must be overloaded on a regular basis with workloads that exceed what is normal for the muscles. If not, changes will not occur.

The benefits of resistance training include:

- Increased muscular strength
- Increased muscular endurance
- Increased lean body mass
- Increased metabolic efficiency
- Increased self confidence and self esteem

- Improved body composition (decreased body fat)
- Increased bone mineral density
- Improved physical appearance

Myths About Resistance Training

Unfortunately, many myths are associated with resistance training. These myths are based on a lack of knowledge in exercise physiology and scientific training principles. Among the most common myths in this regard are the following:

Myth #1: "If not used, muscles will turn to fat."

Certain exercises can improve muscle tone, but those exercises cannot reduce fat in any one specific area. Muscle and fat are different types of body tissue, and the body cannot directly convert one to the other. As an individual exercises to lose body fat, the losses occur throughout the whole body, and not just in the specific area being exercised.

Myth #2: "Consuming large amounts of protein supplements will increase muscle size and strength."

Excess protein will not increase muscle growth, muscle mass, or muscle strength. Approximately 15-20 % of total calories consumed should come from protein-rich foods. The recommended daily allowance (RDA) for protein is 0.8 g/kg of body weight. Using these guidelines, a 165 lb individual (75 kg) would want to consume 60 grams of protein a day. Any additional calories consumed as protein will be converted to fat, and stored.

Athletes may need to consume more protein (i.e., 1.2-1.7 g/kg). Using these guidelines, a 165 lb individual (75 kg) would want to consume 90-128 grams of protein a day.

Myth #3: "Resistance training will make a person muscle bound or inflexible."

A properly designed resistance-training program, one that is performed in the full range of motion, will not result in a decrease in flexibility. In fact, individuals new to exercise will usually increase their flexibility after beginning a resistance-training program. Similarly, people who participate in resistance training may become more muscular, but not muscle bound.

Myth #4: "Resistance training will cause females to get large muscles."

Females lack the hormone testosterone, which is responsible for muscular growth. For this reason, females will not experience the same increases in muscle mass or absolute strength levels as males. With resistance training, females will develop a toned, athletic look. The physiques developed by female bodybuilders can be attributed to genetics, extremely high training volumes (sets x repetitions) and intensities, rigid control of diet, and use of illegal substances.

Myth #5: "Resistance training is only for athletes"

Both athletes and non-athletes alike can benefit from resistance training. Improvements can be seen in muscular strength, muscular endurance, and increased muscular mass (increasing caloric expenditure at rest) with resistance training. Improving these components can help non-athletes in performing activities of daily living.

Types of Resistance Training

Many different methods of resistance training exist. While each method has its advantages and disadvantages, a resistance training program does not need to exclusively utilize one single method.

☐ Free Weights

Free weights consist of dumbbells and barbells. The weights can either be fixed, or interchangeable. The primary advantages that free weights offer are the large variety of exercises and movement patterns that can be performed, and the involvement of stabilizing muscles in performing the exercises. The major disadvantage of free weights is their complicated use compared to other resistance-training methods.

☐ Machines

Resistance training machines usually consist of a lever that moves a weight stack by use of a pulley. The main advantage of machines is their ease of use. The primary disadvantages of machines include larger space requirements, higher cost, and the limited number of exercises that can be performed on each machine.

☐ Body Weight

Body-weight exercises use only the body and gravity for resistance. Examples of body-weight exercises are push ups, pull ups, crunches, and lunges. The main advantage of body-weight exercises is that no equipment is required. The primary disadvantage is the limited number of exercises that can be performed.

☐ Resistance Tubing

Because of the elastic properties of tubing, it can be used for resistance training. Tubing is inexpensive, and can duplicate many machine and free-weight exercises. The main disadvantage of tubing is that as it stretches, it creates more resistance. As a result, an exercise may begin with light resistance, but end with heavy resistance.

Resistance-Training Goals

Resistance training programs can be designed to improve many different physical attributes. While any of the aforementioned listed methods can be used in any program, the repetitions, load, and rest intervals need to be specific to the desired outcome goals.

☐ Strength Training

The fundamental goal of strength training is to develop general strength and power. Strength can be defined as the maximum amount of weight that can be lifted one time. Power is work divided by time, or simply how quickly strength loads can be moved. Programs designed to increase muscular strength are characterized by high intensity (resistance) and low volume (sets multiplied by repetitions). Repetitions will range from 1-6 for strength training, with rest periods of two to five minutes between sets.

☐ Endurance Training

The basic goal of endurance training is to increase muscular endurance. Muscular endurance can be defined as the ability to perform multiple repetitions with a sub-maximal weight. When training for endurance, 12 or more repetitions should be performed, with a rest interval of 30 seconds or less between sets.

☐ Hypertrophy Training

Hypertrophy is defined as an increase in the size of a muscle. Hypertrophy training is designed to increase muscle size. While this form of training is primarily used by bodybuilders, it has applications to athletes. When training for hypertrophy, repetitions should range from 6-12, with rest periods ranging from 30 seconds to a minute and a half.

CHAPTER 2

Exercise Physiology

Keith E. Cinea, MA, CSCS

Motor Units

Every muscle in the human body is made up of thousands of contractile fibers that run the length of the muscle. Each individual fiber within the muscle is connected to a motor nerve. The nerve can innervate as few as five fibers, or more than 150 fibers (Fox, Bowers, & Foss, 1989). The fewer fibers that the nerve innervates, the finer the motor control is. The motor nerve, and all the muscle fibers it innervates, is defined as a motor unit.

When a nerve impulse reaches the motor unit, if the signal is strong enough, it causes all the connected fibers to contract. This factor is called the all-or-nothing principle. It states that if a motor unit receives a signal to contract, it either contracts maximally, or does not contract at all. By varying the number of motor units recruited, the force the muscle produces can be varied.

Along with varying the number of motor units recruited, force generation can be affected by which motor units within a muscle are recruited. The number of muscle fibers within a motor unit will also vary within the muscle itself. One motor unit may only innervate 50 fibers, while another may innervate 100 fibers. Assuming all fibers can generate the same amount of force, the 100-fiber motor unit could generate twice the force that the 50-fiber motor unit could.

The final method for varying force generation within a muscle is called wave summation. When a muscle fiber receives a stimulus from the motor nerve to contract, it responds with a twitch (a brief contraction followed by relaxation). If another impulse to contract is given to the motor unit before it completely relaxes, it will contract again, stronger than before. By summating the contractions, a motor unit can generate greater amounts of force.

Contractions

The most widely accepted theory for how muscles contract is the sliding-filament theory. Inside a muscle fiber there are two contractile filaments, actin and myosin. When the nerve impulse reaches the muscle, it causes the actin and myosin to combine through crossbridges. The crossbridges make it possible for the filaments to slide across each other, shortening the muscle.

Muscle contractions are classified by force generation and the movement they create. The first type of contraction is *concentric*. These contractions are characterized by force generation and a shortening of the muscle. An example of a concentric contraction would be the bicep muscle during the raising phase of a bicep curl.

An *eccentric* contraction is characterized by force generation and a lengthening of the muscle. An example of an eccentric contraction would be the bicep muscle during the lowering phase of a bicep curl.

Isokinetic contractions generate movement (shortening or lengthening of the muscle), however, the speed of the movement is constant. Isokinetic contractions are performed on specialized equipment.

Isometric contractions generate force, but do not produce movement. An example of an isometric contraction is the tricep muscle, while pushing on a wall.

Joint-Movement Patterns

The joints of the human body move in specific patterns. To better understand how muscles move body parts, the following joint movement terminology must be understood:

• Flexion occurs when a joint angle decreases, such as the elbow joint during the raising phase of a bicep curl. The opposite of flexion is extension. Extension involves increasing a joint angle, such as the elbow joint during the lower phase of the bicep curl.

- Abduction is movement away from the centerline of the body. An example of this movement is the shoulder joint during the raising phase of a lateral raise. Adduction is movement towards the centerline of the body. An example of this movement would be the shoulder joint during the lowering phase of a lateral raise.

- Rotation of the hands to a forward or palms-up position is called supination. Rotation of the hands to a backwards or palms-down position is called pronation.

Exercise and Energy Sources

The three major energy systems in the human body are: the phosphagen or immediate system, non-oxidative (glycolysis and glycogenolysis), and oxidative. While all three systems are active at the same time, the percentage of energy used from each system will vary, depending on the intensity and duration of the activity.

The phosphagen system begins all physical activity. Adenosine triphosphate (ATP) is the source of energy that muscles use to contract. However, the muscles contain a very limited supply of this source. Once it is used, the body must replenish it. At the beginning of exercise, this replenishing is done with creatine phosphate (CP). This substance is also limited. If the physical activity is to continue beyond ten seconds, other energy systems must get involved. The phosphagen system is the primary energy system for very high intensity, very short-duration activities such as the shot put, high jump, and long jump.

As physical activity continues, non-oxidative (glycolysis and glycogenolysis) metabolism becomes the dominant energy source. Non-oxidative (anaerobic) activity is of a high intensity, with a short duration. Examples of anaerobic activies include a 100-meter sprint, a maximal squat for 10 repetitions, or stealing second base. The muscles do not require oxygen to perform at this level, but if activity is to be maintained, then the intensity will have to decrease, and oxygen made available to the muscles.

Oxidative (aerobic) activity consists of longer-duration activities and requires oxygen for the muscles. Aerobic activity is long in duration, and lower in intensity. Examples of aerobic activities include cycling and jogging. Aerobic exercise is beneficial in metabolizing fat and increasing energy utilization.

Muscle Adaptations to Training

Endurance training is characterized by repeated contractions of a submaximal load. Traditional endurance activities, such as jogging, swimming, and cycling, have the following two major effects on skeletal muscle: an increase in mitochondrial proteins, and an increase in glycolytic enzymes (Brooks, Fahey, White, 1996). This results in an increased ability for the muscle to perform aerobic metabolism.

Strength training is characterized by low repetitions with a maximal load. Results from strength training include increased motor unit recruitment, and an increase in the size or cross-sectional area of the muscle. The benefit of increased size is that a larger muscle provides a greater capacity for strength and power development (Brooks et al., 1996).

Hypertrophy and Atrophy

Hypertrophy is defined as an increase in the size of the muscle. It is seen as an increase in the cross-sectional area of the muscle fibers. Hypertrophy results from an increase in physical activity, especially an increase in resistance training.

Hypertrophy is caused by an increase in the production of the contractile proteins actin and myosin (Goldberg, Etlinger, Goldspink, & Jablecki, 1975). This factor results in an increase in the number of filaments within the muscle fiber itself, but not an increase in the number of muscle fibers. Increases in the number of human-muscle fibers have yet to be proven in laboratory experiments.

Atrophy is a decrease in the muscle size. This size reduction is usually a result of inactivity, such as casting a broken limb, or a decrease in the amount of physical training.

Muscle Fiber Types

Muscle fibers can be classified by many different methodologies. One of the more popular methods is to classify muscle fibers histochemically. This method involves biopsying muscle samples, incubating them with substrates or stains, and then measuring identifying characteristics.

Fast-twitch, glycolytic (FG) muscle fibers contract quickly, and generate large amounts of force, but fatigue quickly. FG fibers are also high in glycolytic capacity. This means that they are non-oxidative, using anaerobic glucose to provide them with energy.

Slow-twitch, oxidative (SO) muscle fibers contract slowly, and cannot generate as much force as FG fibers, but are resistant to fatigue. SO fibers are oxidative, receiving their energy through aerobic processes. As a result, SO fibers also have a much higher level of mitochondrial density than any other fiber type. Mitochondria are the structures within muscle cells that perform many of the oxidative processes.

Fast-twitch, oxidative glycolytic fibers contract rapidly, generate large amounts of force, and are more resistance to fatigue than FG fibers. They also can use oxidative and non-oxidative processes for energy.

Fast-twitch fibers are better designed for short-duration, high-activity, anaerobic activities. Examples of such activities include weight lifting, shot put, and line blocking in football. Slow-twitch fibers are better suited for endurance or aerobic activities, such as cycling and distance running.

Genetics determine what percentage of each fiber type an individual will have. While endurance training will increase the oxidative capacity of muscle fibers, and sprint training will increase the anaerobic capacity of muscle fibers, training cannot change one fiber type to another (Brooks et al, 1996).

Specificity

Adaptations to a resistance-training program will be specific to the exercise stress. If low-intensity training (such as jogging) is performed, slow-twitch muscle fibers will respond by increasing their oxidative capacity. On the other hand, fast-twitch fibers will have little or no response to this type of training. However, if training is of a high-intensity, low-repetition nature, fast-twitch fibers will respond with hypertrophy and an increase in anaerobic capacity. In this particular situation, the slow-twitch fibers will have little response (Brooks et al, 1996).

Adaptations are specific to the training exercises and muscle groups. For example, in a study by Sale (1988), subjects performed eight weeks of squat exercises. The subjects produced large gains in strength when tested on the squat. When tested on the leg press, which uses the same muscles, their strength gains were about half what they were on the squat. And when tested on the leg extension (which also uses the quadriceps), no gains were seen in strength.

Conclusion

With a basic understanding of how muscles function, and how they adapt to training, the strength coach can design and implement more effective programs. The aforementioned discussion is by no means thorough; it is designed to provide a brief overview for the high school coach.

Muscle Groups: Anatomy and Action

The following chart lists the location of most of the major skeletal muscles that make up the human body. It includes actions and exercises to target the muscles.

Body Part	Muscle	Action	Exercises
Front of upper arm	Biceps brachii Brachialis	Flexion of elbow	Arm curls with palms up
	Brachioradialis	Flexion of the elbow, supination	Arm curls with palms down
Back of upper arm	Triceps Brachii	Extension of elbow	Tricep extension, tricep pushdown
Shoulders	Deltoid (for simplicity this muscle is divided into anterior and posterior fibers only)	Anterior fibers: abduction and flexion of the shoulder joint (arm forward) Posterior fibers: abduction and extension of the shoulder joint (arm backwards)	Anterior fibers: lateral raise, upright row, front raise Posterior fibers: lateral raise, upright row, rear deltoid row
Chest	Pectoralis major	Horizontal adduction, internal rotation of the arm	Bench press, flys
Upper back	Latissimus dorsi	Adduction and extension of the shoulder joint	Pull ups, lat pull down
	Trapezius	Elevation of the shoulders	Shrugs, upright rows
	Rhomboids major Rhomboids minor	Adduction of the scapula	Seated row
Low back	Spinae erector	Extension, rotation and lateral flexion of the spine	Back extension, trunk twists, side bends

Body Part	Muscle	Action	Exercises
Abdominal	Rectus abdominus Internal and external obliques	Flexion of the spine Lateral flexion of spine and spinal rotation	Crunch Side bends, trunk twists
Back of the hip	Gluteus maximus	Extension of the hip	Squat, leg press, hip extension, stiff-leg deadlift
Front of the thigh	Quadriceps • Rectus Femoris • Vastus lateralis • Vastus Medius • Biceps femoris	Extension of knee (Rectus femoris also involved in flexion of the hip)	Leg extension, squats, leg press Rectus femoris: sit up
Back of the thigh	Hamstrings • Semimembranosus • Semitendinosis • Biceps femoris	Extension of the hip and flexion of the knee	Leg curl, squats stiff-leg deadlift
Calf	Gastrocnemius Soleus	Extension of the ankle	Calf raise

CHAPTER 3

Nutrition

Dan Benardot, PhD, RD, LD

Introduction

Producing a strong, well-conditioned athlete involves more than spending long hours in the gym. The nutrition strategies that athletes follow before they get to the gym, what they eat and drink after they leave practice, and what they do to assure an optimal flow of fluid and energy into their bodies during exercise are critical to improving their level of strength, conditioning, and athletic performance.

A failure to consider nutrition as an integral component of the strength and conditioning program will increase the risk for injury and poor health, result in poor improvement rates, and cause a breakdown in the athlete's belief that improvement is possible. On the other hand, well-nourished athletes do better in sports, recover more quickly from unavoidable injuries, and derive more performance-improving benefits from long and strenuous training sessions.

While the scientific information on the relationship between good nutrition and athletic performance is clear, the massive amount of misinformation on sports nutrition often makes it difficult for coaches and athletes to know:

- The best time to eat before practice and competition
- The foods that will best sustain energy levels
- The best fluids to drink before, during, and after competition to assure optimal hydration
- How to balance an optimal energy intake with an ideal body composition
- How to make certain nutrient intake meets nutrient needs

Essential Nutrition Concepts

Nutrients provide muscles with the energy they need to work, help metabolize energy, and provide the building materials for muscles, organs, and bones. For athletes to be healthy and successful in sport, they must think about nutrition needs as having as much importance as training needs.

Nutrients

The six classes of nutrients include:

- Carbohydrates
- Proteins
- Fats
- Vitamins
- Minerals
- Water

Each class of nutrient is important, and athletes should not think of any single nutrient as more critical than any other nutrient. Put simply, nutrient balance is critical to good health and performance. The athlete's goal should be to find the appropriate balance between all the nutrients, since too much or too little of any one nutrient will cause health and/or performance problems.

The easiest way to assure optimal nutrient exposure is to consume a wide variety of foods. Because no single food has all the nutrients a person needs to stay healthy, eating a wide variety of foods helps people know that all the needed nutrients are available to them. An added benefit of eating a wide variety of foods is avoidance of nutrient toxicities, which result from excess vitamin and mineral intake.

The availability of inexpensive nutrient supplements dramatically increases the possibility of nutrient toxicities. Many athletes are motivated by the belief that, 'if a little bit of nutrient is good then more must be better'. There is no evidence that providing more nutrients than the body can use provides a benefit. On the contrary, excess nutrients cause additional energy expenditure to eliminate the surplus.

Nutrition Misinformation

There is a great deal of nutrition information in the media and in health-food stores, making it difficult to make the right choices. Athletes should ask for evidence about whether nutritional products actually work. The best evidence comes from information published in referenced (peer-reviewed) scientific journals.

In seeking nutrition advice, look for people who have a graduate degree in nutrition and/or are Registered Dietitians with the letters "R.D." after their name. Be certain to ask others giving nutrition advice about their formal training in nutrition, and what credentials they have to demonstrate knowledge of sports nutrition.

Energy Nutrients

Energy nutrients are those nutrients that provide fuel for cellular work. Carbohydrates, proteins, and fats are considered energy nutrients because they all can be metabolized as energy. Energy nutrients allow individuals to do muscular work, transfer electrical energy between nerve cells, and maintain body temperature.

Energy is measured in kilocalories. A calorie is a measurement unit in physics. It represents the amount of heat required to raise 1 kg of water 1°C (McArdle, Katch, & Katch, 1999). In the nutrition field, energy is referred to in kilocalories (kcals). A kilocalorie is equal to 1,000 calories.

When a person exercises, the rate at which energy is metabolized rises. Because this process is not 100% efficient, some of the energy is lost as heat. This extra heat causes body temperature to rise, which tells the body to increase its sweat rate as a means of cooling down body temperature. Therefore, the two essential components of sports nutrition are: 1) provision of sufficient extra energy to satisfy the needs of physical activity, and 2) provision of sufficient fluids to maintain body water and replace fluids lost as sweat.

Meeting Energy and Nutrient Needs

All sports have resistance associated with them. Skaters must overcome the resistance of a skate blade going over the ice, cyclists have the resistance created by air, and weight lifters have the resistance from weights. Sports performance is related to the ability of the athlete to overcome resistance (or drag), and the ability to sustain power output by overcoming this resistance on repeated bouts or long distances (Lamb, 1995). While these two factors are clearly related to performance, they are perceived by many athletes to be in conflict—a fact that causes many athletes to have problems with meeting energy needs. Athletes often view their ability to overcome the resistance or drag with their ability to carry a lot of muscle and relatively little fat. Since fat mass does little to contribute to sports performance and may contribute to drag, this reasoning makes lots of sense. However, the strategy that athletes often use to reduce fat mass and maximize muscle mass is to diet by lowering their total energy intake. This dieting strategy is counterproductive, because it restricts the intake of energy that is needed to sustain power output.

How do athletes maximize their ability to sustain power output, while at the same time, reduce body-fat percent to make it easier to overcome resistance or drag? According to a number of studies, the answer may lie in consuming small, but frequent, meals to stay in better energy balance throughout the day (Deutz et al., 2000).

Energy balance has typically been thought of in 24-hour units. That is, if the athlete consumes 3,000 kilocalories during the day and burns 3,000 kilocalories during the day, that individual is in energy balance. However, what athletes do during the day to achieve a state of energy balance makes a difference. If they spend most of the day in an energy-deficit state (metabolizing more kilocalories than are being consumed), but then eat a huge meal at the end of the day to satisfy their energy needs, they might still be in energy balance. It appears that the athlete who does this has different outcomes than the athlete who stays close to an energy-balanced state throughout the day.

Eating small, but frequent, meals has the following benefits:

- Maintenance of metabolic rate
- Lower body fat and lower weight on higher caloric intakes
- Lower blood lipid levels
- Better glucose tolerance and lower insulin response (making it more difficult to manufacture fats from the foods eaten)
- Lower stress hormone production
- Better maintenance of muscle mass
- Improved physical performance

Most surveys of athletes suggest that they tend to delay eating until the end of the day, and many athletes have severe energy deficits earlier in the day (particularly on days when they train hard and need the energy the most!) Problems with energy deficits include:

- Difficulty maintaining carbohydrate stores (this factor would impede endurance on high-intensity activities)
- Problems maintaining lean (muscle) mass
- Lower metabolic rate
- Difficulty meeting nutrient needs (foods carry both energy and other nutrients)
- Increased risk of injury (Undernourished athletes may develop mental and muscular fatigue that, in some sports, would predispose them to injury)
- Missed opportunities to aid muscle recovery

Maintaining energy balance throughout the day by consuming small, but frequent, meals during the day is an excellent strategy for reducing these problems.

Carbohydrates

Carbohydrates are often referred to as if there is only one single carbohydrate compound. In fact, carbohydrates come in many different forms that have different nutritional outcomes. Some carbohydrates are digestible, while others are not; some are considered complex, while others are simple; and some carbohydrates contain soluble fiber, while others contain insoluble fiber. The basic carbohydrate for human nutrition is the simple sugar glucose, but the human body makes a complex carbohydrate called glycogen, which is the storage form of glucose.

▶ Carbohydrate functions

☐ Provide Energy

Carbohydrate is the preferred fuel for the body, and it's an instantaneous energy source. Carbohydrates provide four kilocalories of energy per gram. People should consume at least 40 to 50 grams of carbohydrate per day to avoid health problems. This requirement involves a minimum of between 160 to 200 kilocalories per day from carbohydrates. To assure that they are able to train and compete at their best, athletes should consume carbohydrates well above the following minimum guideline: Athletes should make certain that carbohydrate provides between 55 to 65 percent of their total kilocalories.

☐ Protein Sparing

This factor is an often overlooked, yet very important function of carbohydrates. Because carbohydrate (glucose) is a preferred fuel, providing enough carbohydrate to meet the majority of energy needs preserves protein from being broken down and used as a source of energy. This situation allows protein to be used for important functions that only protein can accomplish, such as building muscle tissue.

☐ Stored Energy

Carbohydrates have two storage forms: glycogen and fat. The ideal storage form for carbohydrate is glycogen, because it can easily be converted back to glucose and used for energy. However the storage capacity for glycogen in the human body is relatively small, so when the glycogen capacity is filled, excess carbohydrate can be converted to and stored as fat.

Examples of Good High Carbohydrate Snacks			
Apple	English muffin	Mashed potatoes	Saltine crackers
Bagel	Fruit cup	Mixed berries	Spaghetti
Baked corn chips	Fruit smoothie	Oatmeal	Whole wheat toast
Baked potato	Gatorade	Orange juice	
Banana	Gatorade energy bar	Popcorn	
Beans	Grapes	Rice	

▶ Types of carbohydrate

☐ Simple Carbohydrates (Sugars)

Simple carbohydrates are sugars that include glucose, fructose (typically found in fruits and vegetables), galactose (one of the sugars in milk), sucrose (table sugar), lactose (milk sugar), and maltose (grain sugar).

☐ Complex Carbohydrates

Complex carbohydrates are carbohydrates that contain many molecules of connected simple carbohydrates. Complex carbohydrates can be digestible (starch, dextrins, and glycogen), or indigestible (cellulose, hemicellulose, pectin, gums, and mucilages).

▶ Carbohydrates in the diet

Should the focus of an athlete's diet be carbohydrate, protein, or fat? There are many studies showing that carbohydrates are the limiting energy substrate for athletes (ACSM, 2000). That is, when carbohydrates run out, the athlete typically reaches a point of exhaustion. It is recommended that athletes consume 55 to 65% of total kilocalories from carbohydrates. For example, an athlete consuming a 3,000-kilocalorie diet should consume between 1,650 to 1,950 kilocalories from carbohydrates. Expressed another way, athletes should consume between 6 to 10 grams of carbohydrate per kilogram of body weight. For a 75-kg (165 lb) athlete, that amounts to between 450 grams (1,800 kilocalories) to 750 grams (3,000 kilocalories) per day from carbohydrate alone.

Ideal Energy Distribution for Athletes

65% from Carbohydrate

15% from Protein

20% from Fat

Carbohydrate is not just for endurance sports. A single 30-second sprint can reduce glycogen storage by over 25%. A high-carbohydrate diet and carbohydrate-containing sports beverages can improve energy reserves and enhance performance of repeated sprints.

Protein

Proteins are large, complex compounds that are made of different amino acids, which uniquely contain nitrogen. Body proteins are constantly changing, with new proteins being made and old ones broken down. Growth hormone, androgen, insulin, and thyroid hormone are anabolic hormones that initiate the formation of new proteins.

Carbohydrate Quick Facts	
Minimum intake	50 to 100 grams per day (200 to 400 kilocalories)
Average U.S. intake	200 to 300 grams per day (800 to 1200 kilocalories per day)
Recommended fiber intake	20 to 30 grams per day, or more
Average U.S. fiber intake	10 to 15 grams per day
Recommended intake of carbohydrate as percent of total caloric intake	55% of total kilocalories; up to 65% of total kilocalories for athletes
Good sources of carbohydrate	Grains, legumes, seeds, pasta, fruits, vegetables

Cortisone, hydrocortisone, and thyroxin are catabolic hormones that initiate the breakdown of proteins.

An athlete's requirement for protein is double that of non-athletes, but most athletes far exceed their need for protein. For instance, the daily non-athlete adult requirement for protein is 0.8 grams per kilogram of body weight, while the adult athlete requirement for protein is between 1.2 and 1.7 grams per kilogram of body weight. An athlete weighing 180 pounds (about 82 kilograms) would require between 98.4 to 164 grams of protein per day. At four kilocalories per gram, this guideline amounts to consuming between 394 and 558 kilocalories from protein per day (Manore & Thompson, 2000). Most athletes far exceed this amount of protein, just from the foods they consume. Consider that the protein in a hamburger, a chicken-fillet sandwich, and one cup of milk provides more than half the total daily protein requirement for a 180-pound athlete.

Examples of Good High Protein Snacks			
Cheese	Hamburger	Soy burger	Yogurt
Tuna sandwich	Cooked beef, lamb,	Milk	Turkey sandwich
Chicken	or pork strips	Cottage cheese	

▶ Protein Functions

☐ Enzyme and Protein Synthesis

There are hundreds of unique tissues and enzymes that are composed of proteins.

☐ Transports Nutrients

Proteins make transportation carriers, enabling nutrients to go to the correct tissues.

□ Source of Energy

The carbon in protein provides the same amount of energy per unit of weight as carbohydrates (four kilocalories per gram).

□ Hormone Production

Hormones control many chemical activities in the body, and are made of unique proteins.

□ Fluid Balance

Protein helps to control the fluid balance between the blood and surrounding tissues. This factor helps athletes maintain blood volume and sweat rates during physical activity.

□ Acid-Base Balance

Proteins can make an acidic environment less acidic and an alkaline environment less alkaline. High-intensity activity can increase cellular acidity (through lactate buildup), which protein can help to buffer.

□ Growth and Tissue Maintenance

Protein is needed to build and maintain tissue. This factor is one reason why the protein requirement for growing children can be double that of adults. The protein requirement for athletes is approximately double that of non-athletes because of muscle development and maintenance, and a small increase in the protein lost through sweat and urine (Williams, 2002). The highest protein requirements are in young, growing athletes.

□ Synthesis of Nonprotein, Nitrogen-Containing Compounds

The compound phosphocreatine is a high-energy nitrogen-containing compound that can quickly release energy over a short duration for quick-burst activities.

▶ **Protein Quality**

Proteins are constructed from amino acids. Amino acids can be classified as either essential or non-essential. The human body can produce essential amino acids, but cannot produce essential amino acids. For this reason, essential amino acids must be consumed in the diet through foods, such as eggs, meats, milk, cheese, and fish.

Athletes frequently take protein supplements, but these often contain proteins with an incomplete set of amino acids, making the supplements low in protein quality. The best protein supplement would be a few pieces of steak or fish. Vegetarian athletes can assure that they consume an optimal protein quality by combining cereal grains (rice, wheat, oats, etc.) with legumes (dried beans or peas.) Vegetarian athletes are clearly more at risk for inadequate protein intake, because the best source of high quality protein is meat and fish. However, with some good diet-planning, vegetarian athletes can consume enough high-quality protein.

Protein is often the focus of the diets of many athletes, but a tendency exists to consume too much protein. Studies have found that athletes do best with protein intakes that supply approximately 15% of total kilocalories or between 1.2 and 1.7 grams of protein per kilogram of body weight. For a 75-kg (165 lb) athlete, that amounts to no more than 150 grams (600 kilocalories) of protein per day (Williams, 2002). Studies have shown that athletes often have protein intakes of more than three grams of protein per kilogram of body weight per day (Manore & Thompson, 2000).

Protein isn't the best fuel for physical activity, but it is a fuel that helps meet energy needs. There is no question that satisfying energy needs must occur before consideration can be given to the best way to distribute carbohydrate, protein, and fat.

Protein Quick Facts	
Recommended intakes	• Infants: 2.2 grams per kg of body weight • Children: 1.0 to 1.6 grams per kg of body weight • Adults: 0.8 grams per kg of body weight • Adult Athletes: 1.2 to 1.7 grams per kg of body weight (strength athletes have a slightly higher requirement than endurance athletes) (Manore & Thompson, 2000)
Recommended intake of protein as percent of total caloric intake	12 to 15% of total kilocalories
Good sources of protein	Meat, poultry, fish, yogurt, eggs, milk; combinations of legumes (beans and dried peas) with cereal grains

Fat

Americans tend to consume too much fat, and now many athletes have the mistaken belief that high fat intakes can enhance athletic performance. The generally accepted limit for fat intake is no more than 30% of total daily kilocalories. For an athlete consuming 2,500 kilocalories per day, this amounts to 750 kilocalories per day as fat (about 83 grams of fat). While this guideline is considered to be the accepted healthy limit, athletes are likely to do better with fat intakes that do not exceed 25% of their daily kilocalories in order to provide more room in their diet for carbohydrates.

▶ Fat Functions

☐ Fats Are a Source of Energy

Fats provide nine kilocalories of energy per gram (compared to four kilocalories per gram from both carbohydrates and proteins).

□ Fat Provides Insulation from Extreme Temperatures and Cushion Against Concussive Forces

Fats protect the body's organs against sudden concussive forces, such as a fall or a solid hit in football. Fats also have excellent insulation capacities.

□ Satiety Control

Because they stay in the stomach longer than other energy nutrients, fats provide a fuller feeling longer.

□ Fat Carries Essential Nutrients

Fats help make sure athletes get the necessary fat-soluble vitamins (A, D, E, and K) and essential fatty acids, which are found in vegetable and cereal oils.

Examples of High Fat Foods			
Whole milk	Nuts	"Crispy" snacks	Margarine, butter,
Pie crust	Fried foods	Regular cheese	lard and oil
High fat dairy products	Peanut butter	Potato chips	

▶ Fat classifications and definitions

Fats and Oils

Fats are solid at room temperature and usually contain a high proportion of saturated fatty acids. Oils are liquid at room temperature and typically (there are notable exceptions) contain a high proportion of unsaturated fatty acids.

□ Triglycerides, Diglycerides, and Monoglycerides

Triglycerides are the most common form of dietary fats and oils, while diglycerides and monoglycerides are less prevalent, but still commonly present in the food supply.

□ Short-Chain, Medium-Chain, and Long-Chain Fatty Acids

The most common dietary fatty acids are long-chain, containing 14 or more carbon atoms. Medium-chain triglycerides (MCT oil) have received some attention recently as an effective supplement for increasing caloric intake in athletes. While MCT oil may hold some promise in this area, it has not been adequately tested.

□ Polyunsaturated Fatty Acids

These fatty acids have a tendency to lower blood cholesterol. The good thing about these fats is that they're typically associated with lots of vitamin E, which athletes need. (Found in vegetable and cereal oil, such as corn oil.)

☐ Monounsaturated Fatty Acids

These fatty acids tend to lower blood cholesterol, while maintaining high-density lipoproteins (HDL). (Found in olive oil and canola oil.)

☐ Saturated Fatty Acids

These fatty acids tend to increase serum cholesterol. (Found in meats and dairy products.)

☐ Low-Density Lipoproteins (LDL)

These lipoproteins are the major carrier of cholesterol and other lipids in the blood.

☐ High-Density Lipoproteins (HDL)

These lipoproteins carry lipids away from storage and to the liver for metabolism and/or excretion. Because they are associated with removal of cholesterol, they are considered good cholesterol.

▶ Fats in the diet

Fats should provide approximately 25 percent of an athlete's total caloric intake. For a 75-kg (165 lb) athlete consuming a 3,000 kilocalorie diet, approximately 600 to 750 kilocalories should come from fat. Because fats provide nine kilocalories of energy per gram, this level of consumption amounts to between approximately 65 to 85 grams of fat per day.

A great deal of attention has been given to high-fat, high-protein, low-carbohydrate diets recently, but little evidence exists that these diets are useful for enhancing athletic performance. In an excellent scientific review of "The Zone and Athletic Performance," it was determined that 'The Zone' diet is (Cheuvront, 1999):

- A calorie-deficient diet by any standard.
- A low-carbohydrate diet (both in relative and absolute terms). A male marathoner weighing 64 kg with 7.5% body fat would have a 1,734-kilocalorie intake following 'The Zone,' while his predicted caloric requirement is more than 3,200 kilocalories.
- Without foundation for claims by proponents of 'The Zone' that it can alter pancreatic hormone response in favor of glucagons.

It is quite true that people on 'The Zone' would lose weight, because it is an energy-deficient intake. However, because athletes must meet their energy requirements to sustain power output, any severely energy-deficient diet, such as 'The Zone,' (whether it is high-fat, high-protein, or high-carbohydrate), is not recommended for optimizing athletic performance.

Fat Quick Facts	
Recommended intakes	Fat intake should provide between 10 to 30% of total kilocalories.
Essential fatty acid	Linoleic acid (and alpha-linoleic acid) is the essential fatty acid, and must be provided in consumed foods. This fatty acid is found in corn, sunflower, peanut, and soy oils.
Carrier of vitamins	Fat is the carrier of the fat-soluble vitamins: vitamins A, D, E, and K.
Calorie dense nutrient	Fats provide more than twice the kilocalories, per equal weight, than carbohydrate and protein (nine kilocalories vs. four kilocalories per gram).
Cholesterol–fat relationship	High fat intakes (not just high cholesterol intakes) result in higher circulating blood-cholesterol levels.
Food sources	Oil, butter, margarine, fatty meats, fried foods, prepared meats (sausage, bacon, salami), and whole-milk dairy products.

Vitamins and Minerals

Vitamins are substances that help essential body reactions take place. The best strategy for assuring an adequate intake of all the vitamins is to eat a wide variety of foods, and consume lots of fresh fruits and vegetables daily. Some vitamins are water soluble, while other vitamins are fat-soluble. The following tables provide a summary of the major vitamins and minerals.

Remember that nutrient balance is a key to optimal nutrition, so athletes should avoid single-nutrient supplementation unless this step has been specifically recommended by a physician to treat an existing nutrient deficiency disease. If a nutrient supplement is warranted because of a poor-quality food intake, athletes should try a multi-vitamin, multi-mineral supplement that provides no more than 100% of the Recommended Dietary Allowance (RDA) for each nutrient. The scientific literature suggests that vitamin and mineral deficiencies are uncommon for athletes, but if they exist, they are most likely for vitamin B-6 and other B-complex vitamins, iron, and calcium, especially when calorie intake is too low to meet energy demands (Benardot et al., 2001).

Water-Soluble Vitamins

Vitamin and Adult Requirement	Functions	Food Sources
Vitamin C 60 mg/day	• Antioxidant • Collagen formation • Iron absorption	Fresh fruits and vegetables. Particularly high in citrus fruits and cherries.
Thiamin (Vitamin B-1) 0.5 mg/1000 kilocalories	• Oxidation of carbohydrates • Nerve conduction	Seeds, legumes, pork, enriched/fortified gains and cereals.
Riboflavin (Vitamin B-2) 0.6 mg/1000 kilocalories	• Oxidation of carbohydrates and fats • Normal eye function • Healthy skin	Milk, liver, whole and enriched grains and cereals
Niacin	• Oxidation of carbohydrates and fats	Enriched grains and cereals.
Vitamin B-6	• Protein synthesis and breakdown • Glycogen breakdown	Meat, fish, potatoes, sweet potatoes, bananas, vegetables
Pantothenic Acid 4 to7 mg/day	• Energy reactions for carbohydrates, proteins, and fats • Fatty acid synthesis	In almost every food (deficiency is very rare)
Biotin 50 to 100 micrograms/day	• Carbon-dioxide transfer (normal respiration)	Egg yolk, nuts, legumes, bacterial synthesis in the gut
Vitamin B-12 2 micrograms/day	• Red blood cell formation	Foods of animal origin and intestinal synthesis. (Pure vegetarians may be at risk for deficiency)
Folic Acid (Folate) ~ 200 micrograms/day	• Cell division • Maturation of red blood cells	Organ meats, green leafy vegetables, whole-grain foods. (This may be the most common vitamin deficiency)

Fluids

Water is a carrier of nutrients to cells, and is the carrier of waste products away from cells. It serves as a body lubricant, and through sweat, helps to maintain body temperature. Lean tissue (muscles and organs) is over 70% water, and about 60%

Fat-Soluble Vitamins

Vitamin and Adult Requirement	Functions	Food Sources
Vitamin A (Retinol) 0.8-1.0 mg/day	• Vision • Growth • Reproduction • Immune Function • Healthy Skin	Fish liver oils, liver, butter, vitamin A+D added milk, egg yolk Pro-vitamin A (Beta-carotene: in dark-green leafy vegetables, yellow vegetables and fruits, and fortified margarines.
Vitamin D 0.01 mg/day	• Calcium absorption • Phosphorus absorption • Mineralization of bone	Fish-liver oils, fortified (A & D) milk, skin synthesis with exposure to light. Small amounts found in butter, liver, egg yolk, and canned salmon and sardines.
Vitamin E 8-10 mg/day	• Powerful antioxidant • Involved in immune function	Vegetable oils, green leafy vegetables, nuts, legumes. (Foods of animal origin are NOT good sources.)
Vitamin K 0.06-0.08 mg/day	• Involved in blood clotting	Green leafy vegetables.

of total body weight is water. Water is so critical to human existence that a failure to supply sufficient water is more likely to cause quick death than a failure to supply any other nutrient.

Water can be lost through breath, skin, urine, sweat, and feces. It is critically important to consume sufficient fluids to maintain body water stores, yet most people rarely stay optimally hydrated. In fact, athletes commonly wait until they become extremely thirsty (indicating a state of dehydration) before they consume fluids.

▶ Meeting fluid needs

A key to athletic success is avoidance of a state of under-hydration. This factor is not as easy as it may seem, because many athletes rely on thirst as the cue for when to drink. Thirst, however, is a delayed sensation that does not occur until the athlete has already lost one to two liters of fluid. Because of this, athletes should learn to consume fluids on a fixed-time interval. Staying optimally hydrated and fueled during exercise has multiple benefits, including (Manore & Thompson, 2000):

Minerals

Vitamin and Adult Requirement	Functions	Food Sources
Calcium ~1,300 mg/day	• Structure of bones and teeth • Blood coagulation • Nerve impulse transmission • Muscle contraction • Acid-base control	Milk and other dairy foods, dark green leafy vegetables, canned fish (with bones), calcium fortified orange juice.
Phosphorus ~1250 mg/day	• Structure of bones and teeth • Component of ATP and other energy-yielding compounds • Acid-base control	Meats, cereals, grains, and dairy products
Iron ~15 mg/day	• Involved in oxygen transfer to cells (hemoglobin in blood; myoglobin in muscle) • In numerous oxidative enzymes	Most absorbable iron: Meats, poultry, fish, egg yolk Less absorbable iron: dark-green vegetables, legumes, peaches, apricots, prunes, raisins
Zinc ~15 mg/day	• Immune system • Wound healing • In over 70 enzymes involved in energy metabolism	Seafood, organ meat, meat, wheat germ, yeast. (Most plant foods are not good sources).
Magnesium ~ 400 mg/day	• Energy metabolism of carbohydrate and fat • Protein synthesis • Water balance • Muscle contractions	Available in many foods, but highest in meats, who grain cereals, seeds, and legumes

- A less pronounced increase in heart rate
- A less pronounced increase in core body temperature
- Improved cardiac stroke volume and output
- Improved skin blood flow (enabling better sweat rates and improved cooling)
- Maintained blood volume
- Reduced net muscle glycogen usage (improving endurance)

The National Athletic Trainers' Association (NATA) has developed the following fluid consumption guidelines (Casa et al., 2000):

☐ Before Training and Competition:	• Drink adequate fluids the day before • Drink at least two cups (17-20 ounces) of fluid two to three hours before exercise or competition
☐ During Training and Competition:	• Replace Sweat Losses • Drink 7-10 oz every 10 to 20 minutes
☐ After Training and Competition:	• Monitor fluid losses • Drink three cups (24 oz) for every one lb weight loss through sweat. (150% of sweat losses should be replaced, because the athlete continues to sweat.) • Rehydrate within two hours post-exercise

What to Look for in a Sports Beverage	
• Six-to seven-percent carbohydrate concentration (approximately 14 grams of carbohydrate per 8 oz) • A combination of sucrose, glucose, and fructose • 50 to 60 kilocalories per 8 oz	• A minimum of 100 mg sodium per 8 oz • A minimum of 28 mg potassium per 8 oz • No carbonation and no caffeine

Considerations for Two-A-Day Practices

According to recent recommendations generated by sports scientists, heat-related deaths in football can be prevented and heat illness-related performance deficits can be reduced if athletes and those working with them take specific actions (GSSI, 2002). The principles for reducing heat-related death and illness that are outlined in this consensus include:

▶ Risks

☐ Heat Acclimation

Poor acclimation to heat and poor cardiovascular fitness are major contributors to heat illness in football players. The first several days of preseason football practice represent the greatest danger for heat-related problems because of inadequate acclimatization and poor fitness.

☐ Dehydration

Large athletes may lose nearly two gallons of sweat during a practice session, but rarely do they adequately replace all the fluid and electrolytes that are lost. It is impossible to adapt to inadequate fluid intake, and as little as a 2% reduction in body weight from fluid loss may predispose an athlete to heat illness. Since football uniforms make it more difficult to dissipate body heat, inadequate fluid intake creates a formula for disaster.

☐ Electrolyte Balance

Sodium can be lost in large quantities through sweat, and unless the sodium is replenished, it becomes impossible to maintain blood volume and sweat rates. This factor makes heat cramps more likely. Consumption of salty snacks and fluids that contain sodium becomes critically important in high heat and humidity environments.

☐ Past History of Heat Illness

Athletes who have experienced heat-related illness in the past may be at increased risk for future heat illness.

☐ Practice Intensity

The intensity of a practice contributes to the risk of heat illness. Regardless of how hot the weather, heat illness can be prevented if the intensity of a practice is low.

☐ Twice-a-Day Practices

These double practices can contribute to heat illness, particularly during the first two days of practice if the athletes do not adequately cool down and hydrate between practices. Athletes who show signs of heat illness at one practice are more likely to be susceptible to a more serious heat illness on subsequent practices.

☐ Dietary Supplements

Supplements containing ephedra or other stimulant drugs may increase body-heat production, and therefore increase the risk of heat illness.

☐ Heat Index

The heat index is a good measure of how hot the environment feels, but is not a good indicator of heat stroke or other heat-related illness in football players. Coaches and sports medicine staff must be alert to signs of heat illness, because no environmental measure exists that can adequately predict risk.

▶ Recommendations

☐ When to Hold Practice

Twice-a-day practices should be held in the coolest parts of the day, and there should be a long rest period between practices. Athletes should be able to adequately cool themselves before the second practice begins. Consideration should be given to alternating days of single and double practices.

☐ Illness and Drugs

Players who are vomiting, have diarrhea, have fevers, are overweight and/or are unfit, or take diuretic drugs or stimulants are a much higher risk for heat illness and should be restricted from playing in the heat or, at the least, monitored carefully.

☐ Uniform

Wearing a full uniform during the first few days of preseason practice in the heat should be avoided. Portions of the uniform should be gradually added over the first week of practice. Whenever possible, players should remove their helmets and raise their jerseys to facilitate heat loss.

☐ Coaching

Players should not be pressured or embarrassed into overexertion by coaches. High-intensity drills should be avoided early in preseason training. If wind sprints (gassers) are done at the end of practice, they should be done without helmets and pads, and athletes should be carefully monitored for signs of heat illness.

☐ Hydration and Electrolyte Balance

Education of the dangers of heat illness and the importance of proper hydration should be a primary focus for players throughout the season. Parents, coaches, and sports-medicine staff should monitor the fluid intake of players to assure adequate fluid consumption, and frequent breaks should be scheduled to offer players an opportunity to hydrate and to cool themselves in shaded areas with fans. Before and after practice, players should be weighed to monitor fluid loss. Players who experience significant weight loss (more than 1% of body weight) should be counseled and monitored to improve fluid intake during practice.

Early Detection of Heat Illness

All football teams should have immediate access to a certified athletic trainer to educate players about heat illness, to detect signs of heat illness, and to initiate emergency treatment if needed. Sports-medicine staff (team physician, athletic trainer, etc.) should have the authority to remove players from practice if heat illness is suspected. This stipulation should not be under the authority of the coach unless no sports medicine staffs are present.

Warning Signs of Dehydrations, Heat Exhaustion and Heat Stroke

- Dehydration with loss of energy and performance
- Dehydration with muscle cramps
- Heat exhaustion with dizziness, light-headedness, and cold, clammy skin
- Heat exhaustion with nausea/headaches
- Heat stroke with high body temperature and dry skin
- Heat stroke with confusion or unconsciousness

Adapted from: Fluids 2000, The Gatorade Company®

Guidelines for Eating and Drinking Before, During, and After Exercise

▶ **Before exercise or competition**

The pre-exercise meal should focus on the provision of carbohydrates and fluids. Ideally, athletes should consume a high-carbohydrate, low-fat meal three hours before exercising or before competition. Light carbohydrate snacks (crackers, etc.) and carbohydrate containing beverages can be consumed after the meal and before exercise, provided large amounts are not consumed at one time. The athlete should drink 17 to 20 ounces of fluid two to three hours before practice or competition, and an additional seven to ten ounces of fluid 10 to 20 minutes before practice or competition.

▶ **During exercise or competition**

The athlete should drink 28 to 40 ounces of fluid (sports beverages containing a 6-to-7 percent carbohydrate solution and electrolytes are preferred) per hour. This recommendation corresponds to about seven to ten ounces every 10 to 15 minutes, but this amount may need to be adjusted based on body size, sweat rate, exercise intensity, and environmental conditions. Two main goals of this guideline are to avoid dehydration and to avoid the mental and muscular fatigue that can be caused by inadequate carbohydrate replacement.

▶ **After exercise or competition**

Muscles are receptive to replacing stored glycogen following exercise. Because of this factor, athletes should consume 200 to 400 kilocalories from carbohydrates immediately following activity, and then an additional 200 to 300 kilocalories from carbohydrates within the next several hours.

Athletes should drink at least 20 ounces of fluid per pound of body weight that was lost during the practice or competition. These fluids should be consumed within two hours of finishing the practice or competition, with the goal of returning body weight to near pre-exercise weight before the next exercise bout.

CHAPTER 4

Program Design

Michael Barnes, MEd, CSCS

Program design refers to how training variables and administrational concerns are merged together to meet the goals of the particular program. Not all programs will be created the same for each sport or athlete; the specific features of a particular program will depend on the need analysis on which the program is based. Changes in the program will vary throughout the year, and it is the responsibility of the strength and conditioning coach to determine the appropriate course of action.

This chapter is divided in two parts. The first part addresses the components of the program design, while the second section presents the periodization model.

Before Getting Started

▶ **Classroom and administrative concerns**

Selection or determination of the size of a class is dependent upon numerous variables, including the overall size and layout of the facility, the amount of equipment, exercise selection, the number of supervisors available, experience of the students, etc.

The school administration and the teacher should each review these considerations to determine the desired student-to-teacher ratio. The National Strength and Conditioning Association's Professional Standards and Guidelines recommend that a 10:1 student to instructor ratio not be exceeded. This ratio takes into consideration the experience, safety, and maturity of the student into account.

Oftentimes, the high-school facility may be limited in space. As a result, to better assist with traffic flow and use of equipment, it maybe advantageous to split the class into two groups. Each group could then have a different training routine, utilizing different floor space and training equipment.

▶ Personal planning for the student

Goal Setting for the student can serve as motivation and inspiration. Students tend to have different motivations for resistance training, such as improved physical appearance, increased sport performance, increased body weight, reduced body fat, improved confidence, etc. Accordingly, the coach can use goal setting as a tool to track how the program is progressing and its effectiveness for each particular student.

The student and coach should sit down together on a scheduled basis to determine short-, intermediate-, and long-term goals. Setting goals that are realistic is important. Setting goals that are too high can be a source of frustration and could possibly result in dropping out of the training program. On the other hand, setting goals that are too low may compromise the results that are achieved from the program.

▶ Establishing limitations

It is important to determine the medical history of each student prior to that individual engaging in the training program. The strength and conditioning coach must require athletes to undergo health-care provider screening and clearance prior to participation. Specific preparticipation screening and clearance is defined in the National Strength and Conditioning Association's Professionals Standards and Guidelines (Appendix A).

As a result of the preparticipation screening and clearance, an athlete may be determined to have physical limitations. If so, the sport coach, physician, athletic trainer, parent, athlete, and strength and conditioning coach should all be aware of the player's condition and the necessary course of action that should be taken concerning that condition in all circumstances.

Components of Program Design

Needs Analysis

The needs analysis should be completed prior to designing the training program for a particular athlete. Table 4-1 illustrates a sample form that coaches should use to conduct their needs analysis. In this stage, several factors should be considered, including:

- An analysis of the fitness needs of both the activity and the individual involved in the sport.

- A physiological and biomechanical analysis that will help enable a program to be designed that addresses the aspects of agility, balance, coordination, strength, flexibility, power, endurance, and speed.

- A biomechanical analysis that will allow training activities to be selected that develop the athlete in the manner most specific to the sport, and also will help identify the areas of critical stress on the athlete's body.

- A discussion of each athlete's injury profile with the medical personnel should be performed to determine the individual's specific needs, with regard to injury prevention.

Once the needs analysis has been completed, the strength and conditioning coach should be able to answer the following questions:

☐ What is the basic energy system profile of the sport?
- ✓ Phosphagen: 0-6 seconds
- ✓ Non-oxidative: Up to two to three minutes in duration
- ✓ Oxidative: Over 2-3 minutes

☐ What are the movements which must be trained?
- ✓ Flexion
- ✓ Extension
- ✓ Linear movements
- ✓ Lateral movements

☐ What are the most common injury sites?
- ✓ Muscles
- ✓ Tendons and ligaments
- ✓ Joints
- ✓ Specific areas (e.g., low back, calf, shoulder, etc.)

Table 4-1. A sample needs analysis form

ATHLETE'S NAME:
DATE:
SPORT:
SPORT ANALYSIS:

DESCRIPTION OF SPORT:

MOST COMMON INJURIES:

MOVEMENTS THAT MUST BE TRAINED:

POSITION PLAYED:
PHYSIOLOGICAL DESCRIPTION OF THE ATHLETE:
Evaluator:

	Previous year:	Present year:
Height	_____	_____
Weight	_____	_____
Girth Measurements		
• Neck	_____	_____
• Chest	_____	_____
• Biceps	___ ___	___ ___
• Forearm	___ ___	___ ___
• Waist	_____	_____
• Hip	_____	_____
• Thigh	___ ___	___ ___
• Calf	___ ___	___ ___
Body Composition		

TEST RESULTS:

Flexibility
Test: _____ Results: _____
_____ _____

Agility and Speed
Test: _____ Results: _____
_____ _____

Muscular Strength
Test: _____ Results: _____
_____ _____

Aerobic Power
Test: _____ Results: _____
_____ _____

Anaerobic Power
Test: _____ Results: _____
_____ _____

Local Muscular Endurance
Test: _____ Results: _____
_____ _____

AREAS THAT NEED IMPROVEMENT:
(Coaches use only)

Program-Design Variables

Program design variables are important factors that influence training adaptations. Program goals and the needs analysis will determine how the design of the program addresses such program-design variables as rest intervals, sets, repetitions, frequencies, how much weight is lifted, and the length of the training sessions. The basic program variables that should be considered when designing a resistance program are discussed in the following sub-sections:

Number of repetitions

The number of repetitions (i.e., how many times a particular exercise is performed per set) can be used to help determine what the training goals are and whether they are being met. As a general rule of thumb, the higher the repetitions (more than 10), the more emphasis will be placed on muscular endurance. The fewer the repetitions, the greater the emphasis on muscular strength.

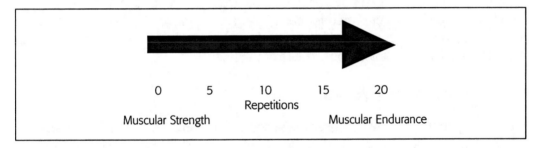

The number of repetitions will change as the program progresses through the athlete's training cycle. Periodization will be defined later in the chapter, but if the individual is using a linear periodization model, the trend is from higher repetitions to lower over the period of time.

More technical movements, like the power snatch and power clean, should be performed with fewer repetitions, and as a general guideline, with no more than six repetitions. A higher repetition for the assistive movements (pulls) of the full Olympic exercises is acceptable, if the proper mechanics for performing these exercises are not sacrificed.

The number of repetitions that should be performed is usually different for core exercises and auxiliary exercises. Core movements, like squats, barbell benches, power cleans, and power snatches, are generally performed with fewer repetitions in the same training session than the assistant movements. For example, if the selected number of repetitions for squats is six, then the number of repetitions for the assistant exercises, like lunges, should be eight. This general trend will usually exist for the entire training cycle.

▶ Number of sets

A set is performing a prescribed number of repetitions on a consecutive basis, before resting. For strength development, three to six sets at the target weight/intensity have proven to be most productive. This has been a point of contention with different training methodologies and philosophies. Considerable research, however, has shown that performing multiple sets is best for strength and power gains (Baker, Wilson, & Carlyon, 1994; Fleck & Kraemer, 1997; Koziris, 1995; Kramer, et al., 1997; Kraemer 1997; Stone, et al., 1998; Stowers, et al., 1983; Willoughby, 1993).

Generally, it is recommended that more sets of core exercises be completed than assistant exercises. Since the loads used for core exercises are higher, build-up or progression sets are needed to reach these higher intensities. Furthermore, because the greatest degree of training effect/adaptation comes from the core exercises, athletes should spend most of their efforts maximizing this effect.

The number of sets prescribed for each exercise will also be influenced by the amount of time needed and available for a particular workout. Clearly, the higher the number of repetitions performed for each exercise, the longer it will take to complete the training session. In addition, the higher the number of repetitions performed, the longer it takes for the athlete to recover from the set.

Time available for the workout

Depending on the circumstances, some schools have more time available for working out than others. The length that a particular workout will involve can be determined once the total number of sets and rest periods have been identified. The coach should keep in mind that each repetition will take a specific amount of time. With regard to developing a time-efficient program, one effective technique that the strength and conditioning coach may consider is to group the athletes together in threes. While one athlete is performing their set, the other two are recovering. This technique is used most effectively with higher-level athletes who are sufficiently skilled to maintain the rhythm or tempo of a training session. In this regard, if thinking about using groups of three to train, the coach should consider several factors before reaching a decision, including how much recovery time each athlete will need, how well an individual has mastered the techniques involved in the training, etc.

▶ Rest and recovery

Considerable attention has been paid to the rest and recovery of athletes. The faster the individual can recover from a training session, the greater the potential there is for more intense training. Several factors may effect how an individual recovers, including:

- *Age:* Generally the older the individual, the longer it will take to recover.
- *Experience:* The higher the experience level, the more efficient the exercises

become. Furthermore, the more experience that individuals have, the better level of their conditioning and ability to recover.

- *Gender:* May affect recovery mainly due to differences between the endocrine systems of males and females.

- *Environment:* As a general rule, the higher the heat and humidity, the lower the ability to recover.

- *Emotional state:* Stress has a negative effect on the ability to recover.

- *Fatigue:* Work performed during the training session has an accumulative effect and can impair recovery, especially for the beginning exerciser.

- *Nutritional status:* Replenishment of nutrients (proteins, fats, and carbohydrates) at the cellular level also affects the recovery process.

▶ Selection of exercises

An infinite number of exercises exist that can be selected when designing a program. Each exercise has certain advantages and disadvantages. From an administrational perspective, strength coaches should never teach an exercise with which they are not completely comfortable.

Resistance training can be performed with either machines or free weights. Machines can be costly, and most often, can only serve to train one movement. On the other hand, training exclusively with free weights is best undertaken with the assistance of a strength and conditioning coach who has a relatively high degree of knowledge. Furthermore, the coach/athlete interaction is much greater when training with free weights than with machines.

☐ Machines and Free Weights

- *Machines.* Training for athletics with machines has both advantages and disadvantages. One of the advantages of machines is their ease of use. Machines do not require an in-depth knowledge of multi-joint, closed-chain (where the foot is on the ground), functional exercises. The major mechanics of the movements are determined by the machine. For instance, when using a selectorized or plate-loaded machine, the path of movement is determined by the machine, which is usually a one-dimensional plane. On the other hand, free weights offer movement in three dimensions: forward/backward, up/down, and left/right (sagital, frontal, and transverse planes). Furthermore, training with machines does not give individuals (of all ages) the opportunity to create the multiplicity of motor patterns that are possible (and desirable) with the use of free weights. In addition, machine training does not enhance intermuscular coordination, require balance, or transfer external forces in a functional manner.

- *Free weights.* Training with free weights is ideal for functional application not only in sport, but also in daily activity. Many movements in athletics require transferring force from the ground to an implement or external resistance. For instance, throwing, tackling, kicking, and wrestling are examples of this principle. Performing ground-based lifts, like the Olympic movements, squats, and all their variations, are examples of transferring force from the ground to an external resistance. This attribute is one of the basic reasons for using free weights.

☐　Single-joint and Multi-joint Exercises

Performing single-joint exercises can isolate muscle groups and potentially concentrate on weaker body parts. These exercises may be beneficial for the injured athlete who may not be able to do closed-chain, multi-joint movements. On the other hand, coaches should remember that choosing to use single joint exercises traditionally takes considerably longer to train the entire body and may require many different types of equipment.

Structural exercises use multiple joints (involving more that one joint in a dynamic manner), and usually involve contact with the floor with one or both feet (closed chain). Examples of this type of exercise include power cleans, squats, lunges, and standing push presses. As rule, these movements are done with free weights. Multi-joint exercises have the following advantages and disadvantages:

Advantages of Multi-joint Exercises:

- Best for strength, power and size gains.
- Involve large muscle masses.
- Have a high degree of inter-and intramuscular coordination.
- Many muscle groups working together emulates the sequential movement athletes utilize on the field.
- Muscles are well balanced in strength.
- Reduce workout time.
- Have the greatest effect on the endocrine system.

Disadvantages of Multi-joint Exercises:

- Require more coaching and supervision.

Single-joint movements further isolate specific muscle groups, and only one joint moves. These movements can be performed with free weights or machines. Examples of these movements include: bicep curls, knee extensions, dumbbell side raises and hamstring curls. Single-joint movements have the following advantages and disadvantages:

<u>Advantages of Single-joint Exercises:</u>

- Good for beginning stages of injury rehabilitation.
- Require less supervision.
- Produce a specific training effect to specific muscle group.

<u>Disadvantages of Single-joint Exercises:</u>

- Little application to activity.
- May require expensive, single-purpose equipment.
- Have little effect on the endocrine system.
- Increase training time for workouts.
- May develop muscle-strength imbalance.
- Muscles do not work in a coordinated fashion.

A multitude of different ways exist to classify exercises, such as isotonic, isokinetic, isometric, variable resistance machines, selectorized machines, and plate-loaded machines. Over the years, the fitness-equipment manufacturing industry has combined many of these aspects into different training devices. These devices all operate on the concept of overloading the body with resistance. In the final analysis, the coach must determine which exercises are most appropriate for his school's situation. The *NSCA's Essentials of Strength and Conditioning* text is an excellent reference to further define exercise types and classifications.

▶ Order of exercises

The order of exercises refers to the sequence in which exercises are preformed in a training session. The order of exercises provides the basic framework for the workout and as much, significant implications exist when ordering exercises. Properly ordering exercises can ensure the greatest training effect, maximize technique, minimize fatigue, and minimize the potential for injury.

If the program that has been designed involves selecting exercises and performing one or more sets before going to the next exercise, three basic concepts should be kept in mind:

- Start with large, multi-joint movements and progress to single-joint movements.
- Start with high-technique movements and move to less-technical movements.
- Start with fast movements and go to slow movements.

With regard to determining how the exercises should be ordered in a particular resistance-exercise program, the high school strength coach may want to consider the following less commonly employed approaches to training:

☐ Pre-Exhaustive Training

This method pre-exhausts assistive or synergistic muscles before training the larger muscle masses. As an example, perform tricep press downs and front shoulder raises before bench pressing. The theory behind this approach to training is to fatigue the assistive muscles first. That step will lead to a greater training effect/effort by the large muscle masses that are activated later. The drawback to this method is that it can often lead to mental and physical fatigue before training the larger muscle-mass movements, resulting in less resistance being used. Researchers have studied this method and discovered that the training loads were significantly reduced when compared to a non pre-exhaustive method (Fleck & Kraemer 1997).

☐ Circuit Training

Circuit weight training places exercises in a sequence, with minimal rest intervals between movements. How many stations are used, the time between exercises, how long the training and rest interval should be, the exercise section, and the order of exercises are among the factors that need to be addressed when planning a circuit resistance-training program. Circuits can be arranged in various ways, depending on needs analyses. The possible combinations are endless, including the following:

- Alternate upper and lower body exercises.
- Combine upper and lower body exercises.
- Combine push or pull exercises.
- Integrate metabolic training, such as stationary cycling or rope jumping, with resistive-training exercises.

▶ **Duration**

Duration refers to the length of time of a specific exercise or exercise session. For example, a particular resistance-training session might last for an hour or a 4 mile-run might take 36 minutes. As such, the strength and conditioning coach must be aware of and address several administrative concerns when determining the duration of the training session, including the following:

- Times of the day the weight room is available
- Number of athletes training at the same time (increased numbers may lead to a longer duration of training)
- Fitness levels of students
- Class scheduling

▶ **Frequency**

Frequency of training is the recurrence of training sessions per day, week, and month.

Frequency of training will be determined by such training factors as the individual's fitness level, the number and scheduling of sport practice sessions, the time of year, and the specific goals of the resistance-exercise training program. For example, high-level athletes can train and usually effectively recover from working out multiple times per day. This level of training takes careful planning and requires the athlete to have several years of intense physical-training experience. At the high-school level, however, strength and conditioning training should be considered on a once-a-day basis—at least initially.

Resistance training and conditioning frequency will typically be reduced when the athlete is competing in-season. The reason for this reduction is that most of the student's energy should be focused on competing and practice. However, in order to maintain hard-earned gains in strength and conditioning during the season, structured strength and conditioning sessions should still be maintained. The general approach should be to do as little as possible in order to maintain strength and conditioning, but no less.

▶ Volume

Volume is the amount of training performed in a particular work period. It is quantified in weight training as being proportional to the load (repetitions x weight). For example, four sets of 10 repetitions represents a volume of 40.

Volume is one index of physiological stress. As such, the fitness level of the athlete is directly proportional to the amount of volume he will be able to tolerate. This factor has significant impact when training students of different ages and grade levels on the same team. As such, an older, more experienced athlete will be able to tolerate greater loads than a less-experienced individual.

Recovery between sessions involving high volumes of training is critical to ensure sufficient recovery before subsequent training. Adequate recovery from high volumes of training will also reduce the likelihood of injury.

▶ Intensity

One of the most misunderstood concepts in training is intensity. Intensity refers to the quality of effort—a factor that can be defined in several different ways, including:

- Strength: expressed in terms of 1 repetition max (RM) or multiple RMs.
- Endurance/speed: expressed as % of VO₂Max, % of HR max, meters/sec, stride rate, time or distance.
- Jumping/throwing: expressed in height or distance.

It is important for coaches to keep in mind that adding too much resistance/ intensity too quickly can lead to overtraining and increase the potential for injury. This mistake of adding too much intensity is often observed when an athlete joins his teammates midway through a training cycle. As a consequence, minimal gains will be typically made, thereby ending up in frustration for both the athlete and coach.

Periodization

Periodization is the process of systemizing training variables to elicit the greatest possible desired effect. Periodization was developed to optimize peak performance at a specific time in the training year, usually to correspond with the athlete's most important competition (state, nationals, Olympics, etc).

Periodization has three distinct phases or cycles—the macrocycle, the mesocycle and the microcycle:

- *Macrocycle*—overall training period. This period usually involves the entire training year, but it can also refer to a period of many months to as much as four years, (e.g., involving a single, entire Olympic training period).
- *Mesocycle*—contained within a macrocycle. Generally, each macrocycle contains two or more mesocycles. This phase may last from many weeks to several months, depending on the goals of the athlete and the number of competitions contained within the period.
- *Microcycle*—daily and weekly variations in volume, intensity, loading and exercise selection. Generally, this cycle involves 1-week (7 days) periods of training.

A mesocycle can further be broken down into three distinct phases; the *preparatory period* (or off-season), the *competition period* (or in-season) and the *transition period*, which begins at the conclusion of the in-season. The specific goals of the cycle and the amount of time between competitions dictate the time spent on each period. Each phase has its own distinct characteristics and parameters.

▶ **Preparatory period:**
- Because no important competitions are conducted during this phase, the major emphasis is on conditioning, with sport-specific skill practices, and few game-strategy sessions.
- Conditioning activities are begun at relatively low intensity and high volume.
- Long, slow distance running or swimming could be appropriate.
- Low-intensity plyometrics are performed.
- High-repetition weight training is done with light-to-moderate resistance.
- Activities progress in weekly microcycles that gradually add intensity, while lowering volume.

With resistance training, the preparatory period involved four phases—hypertrophy, strength, power, and peaking. Each of these phases features a different combination of the volume and intensity training variables:

- ☐ Phase I – Hypertrophy:
  - Highest volume (3-5 sets of 8-20 repetitions)
  - Lowest intensity (50% - 75% of 1 RM)

- ☐ Phase II – Basic strength:
  - Moderate volume (3-5 sets of 5-8 repetitions)
  - Moderate intensity (80% - 90% of 1RM)

- ☐ Phase III – Power Phase:
  - Low volume (3-5 sets of 3-5 repetitions)
  - High intensity (90% - 95% of 1RM)

- ☐ Phase IV – Peaking phase:
  - Lowest volume (2-3 sets of 3-5 repetitions)
  - Highest intensity (90%-100% of 1 RM)

Chart 4-1 iillustrates how variables will change throughout a program.

Chart 4-1. Preparatory phases during resistance training

Variables	Hypertrophy	Basic Strength	Power	Peaking
Sets	3-6	3-5	3-5	2-3
Reps	8-20	5-8	3-5	3-5
Days/wk	3-4	3-5	3-5	1-5
Times/day	1-3	1-3	1-2	1
Intensity Cycle (weeks)	2-3/1	2-4/1	2-3/1	1-3
Duration	60min	50min	45min	30min
Intensity	Low	Moderate to High	High	High
Volume	High	Moderate to High	Low	Very low

► **Competition period:**

- Begins with a shift to very high intensity work with low volume.

- Practice in skill technique and game strategy increases dramatically, as strength and conditioning work decreases proportionally.

- The primary goal of this period is for athletes to reach their highest level of fitness and performance in order to prepare them for their most important competitions.

► **Transition period:**

- Begins with a period of active rest lasting one to four weeks, depending on the length of season.

- Involves little formal or structured training.

- Involves participation in recreational activities, primarily to enable athletes to recover from the stresses of the competition period, to help avoid overtraining, and help enable them to prepare for a new training period.

- Examples of activities that are performed in this period include: racquetball, swimming, and other general fitness activities, performed in a leisurely manner.

Experience using periodizations models will assist coaches with their particular programs. Unforeseen difficulties and problems will arise that will have to be evaluated, and decisions will need to be made, which experience can help the coach to make in a more thoughtful, informed way.

CHAPTER 5

Warm-Up, Stretching and Flexibility

Randy Best, MBA, CSCS, *D
Keith E. Cinea, MA, CSCS
Bruce Harbach, CSCS, *D

The warm-up increases core body temperature and prepares the body for exercise. It may be formal (mimicking the actual activity about to take place), or general (consisting of activities not related to the impending activity itself). The warm-up should be progressive in nature, beginning slowly with a gradual increase in tempo. General warm-up activities include but are not limited to: stationary bike riding, brisk walking, rope jumping, elliptical trainers, jogging, etc. Formal warm-ups mimic a specific sport activity—e.g. shooting baskets, throwing a baseball, hurdle drills, etc. (Baechle & Earle, 2000; Baechle & Grooves, 1972).

Once the muscles have warmed up, stretching exercises can be performed. This sequence decreases the likelihood of injuries that can occur when stretching a cold muscle. In this context, a muscle can be compared to a rubber band. If the rubber band is placed in a freezer, then taken out and immediately stretched, it will break. But if the same rubber band is taken out and warmed up, it will stretch with less chance of breaking.

Stretching and flexibility exercises should be an integral part of every workout, both before and after workouts. Flexibility exercises may be static (positions held with very little movement) or dynamic (slow movements, without bouncing or resistance of a joint to movement) (*Make the Play*, 1998).

Range of motion (ROM) is described as the entire movement through which a body part rotates around a joint. Muscles must be taught to work through a full range of motion. ROM may be improved by engaging in a systematic flexibility program.

Benefits of the Warm-Up

Warming up prior to strenuous exercise will help prepare the athlete both physically and mentally to train at peak performance. The warm-up should concentrate on the major muscle groups, specifically the hamstrings, quadriceps, muscles of the low back, calves, neck, and shoulders (Baechle & Earle, 2000; Baechle & Grooves, 1972; McFarlane, 1987). The warm-up should be progressive, starting slow with gradual increases in tempo. The specific benefits of the warm-up may include, but are not limited to (Baechle & Grooves, 1972; McFarlane, 1987):

- Increase range of motion in joints
- Decrease the viscosity of joint fluids
- Increase muscle core temperature
- Increase heart rate, therefore increasing the volume of blood flow to muscles
- Warm up muscles, tendons and ligaments
- Decrease the chance of severe injury to muscles, ligaments, tendons, and joints

Factors That Affect Flexibility

Flexibility is not the same from person to person or joint to joint within the same individual. Variability in flexibility can be affected by any or all of the following factors:

- *Age*—Flexibility decreases with age, due to changes in elasticity and deceases in physical activity.
- *Gender*—Evidence suggests that females are more flexible than males. Among the factors involving women that may account for such differences are less muscle mass, pelvic structure, and hormones (especially during pregnancy).
- *Physical activity*—Lack of physical activity results in a decrease in flexibility due to shortening of the muscle. Using the muscles in the same activity pattern or maintaining the same posture (e.g., sitting at a desk) may result in tightness and shortening of the muscle.

- *Temperature*—As the temperature of the joint and muscle increases, the range of motion increases.

Types of Stretching Exercises

Stretching exercises can be classified into three different types—static, ballistic, and dynamic. Static flexibility exercises involve a passive stretch, where the stretch is held in one position for a predetermined time (usually 15-30 seconds). This method is the most common type of flexibility exercise.

Ballistic stretches are characterized by bouncing, rapid stretches, where momentum carries the body or body segment through the ROM. An increased risk of injury exists with ballistic stretches, because these stretches work against the muscle's stretch reflex (the characteristic inside the muscle that works to prevent it from being over-stretched). For this reason, ballistic stretches should not be performed.

Dynamic stretches use functional exercises, based on sport-specific movements to prepare the body for activity. These exercises are usually performed during the specific warm-up.

Frequency and Duration of Warm-Up

A warm-up should precede any physical activity. It should begin with a general warm-up, consisting of 5-10 minutes of light aerobic type activity (walking, jogging, cycling, etc).

The second phase of the warm-up is the specific warm-up. This phase, consisting of movements similar to the movements seen in the sport or activity, should last between 8-12 minutes. The specific warm-up period is when dynamic flexibility exercises would be performed. For example, after a general warm-up, a baseball player might progress into rotational, warm-up movements that mimic the motion of swinging a baseball bat, and into shoulder movements similar to throwing a ball.

Five Steps to Static Stretching

- Move the body or body part into the stretching movement. This period is the easy-stretch phase.
- From the easy stretch, slowly increase the intensity of the stretch and hold from 10 to 20 seconds. This phase involves developmental stretches.
- Hold the position, and do not bounce while stretching.
- Stretch to the point of pain. This period is the drastic stretch phase. If pain is felt, slowly move away from the position.
- Relax while stretching (McFarlane, 1987).

Common Static Stretches

Standing Quadricep Stretch

From a standing position near a wall, flex the knee, and bring one foot up behind the body. Grasp the foot with the hand of the same side, using the other hand for balance. Keep the knee pointed toward the ground and the hip over the knee. Repeat with the other leg.

Standing Calf Stretch

From a standing position near a wall, stager the feet so that one foot is in front of the other. Keeping the rear heel on the ground, lean forward into the wall; do not bend at the knee or hip. Repeat with the other leg in back. This exercise stretches the gastrocnemius. To stretch the soleus muscle (which lies underneath the gastrocnemius), bring both feet together, and stand closer to the wall. Repeat the stretch, but bend at the knees.

Chest Stretch

Using a doorway or outside corner, place one arm on the wall, with a 90-degree bend at both the elbow and shoulder. Keeping the chest up, rotate the torso and legs away from the corner until a stretch is felt in the chest. Repeat on the other side. This exercise stretches the pectoralis muscle group.

Tricep and Latisimus Dorsi Stretch

From a standing position, point one elbow toward the ceiling. The hand should fall onto the back. Place the other hand on the back of the elbow, and apply light pressure backwards until a stretch is felt in the tricep and the latisumus dorsi. Repeat on the other side.

Back Stretch

From a standing position, bring one arm across the front of the body. With the opposite arm, grab the back of the elbow, and pull the arm towards the body. Repeat with the opposite side. This exercise stretches the upper back.

Modified Hurdler's Stretch

From a seated position, bend one knee so that the sole of the foot is against the inside of the opposite thigh. While facing the straight leg, bend at the waist, and reach toward the toes. This exercise stretches the hamstrings, gluteals, and low back.

Rotational Stretch

From the modified hurdler's stretch position, place the foot of the bent leg on the outside of the straight leg. Rotate in the direction of the bent leg, using the arm of the opposite side to assist in stretching. Repeat on the other side. This exercise stretches the low back and hip.

Sample Dynamic Warm-Up Exercises

Walking Arm Circles

While walking over a distance of 20-30 yards, perform giant arm circles. These should be performed slowly with control. Bring the arms from a position beside the body to a series of points—behind the body, above the head, in front of the body, and back to the sides. Repeat the exercise, performing the arm circles in the opposite direction.

Walking Knee Tucks

From a standing position, step forward with the right leg. Bring the left knee up to the chest, using the hands to assist. Pause in the top position, then release the leg, and repeat on the other side. Try to pull the knee higher on each repetition. Perform over a distance of 20-30 yards.

Lunge Walk

With the hands clasped behind the head, lunge out with the right leg. Be sure to keep the chest up, the knee of the right leg behind the toes, and the knee of the left leg off the ground. Rise up, bringing the left leg even with the right, and then repeat the exercise, leading with the left leg. Perform over a distance of 20-30 yards.

Reverse Lunge Walk

With the hands clasped behind the head, step backwards with the left foot. Keeping the head and chest up, squat down into a lunge position. Be sure the knee of the right leg does not extend beyond the toes, and that the knee of the left leg does not touch the ground. Rise up, keeping the chest and head up. Bring the right leg even with the left, and repeat the exercise leading with the right leg. Perform over a distance of 20-30 yards.

Walking Side Lunge

With the hands clasped behind the head or in front of the body for balance, take a lateral step to the left. Keeping the right leg straight, sit back with the hips. Be sure to keep the knee of the left leg from extending beyond the toes. Perform over a distance of 20-30 yards, and then repeat, leading with the right leg.

Walking Lunge Twist

With the hands clasped behind the head, lunge out with the right leg. Be sure to keep the chest up, the knee of the right leg behind the toes, and the knee of the left leg off the ground. In the bottom position, rotate the trunk so that the left elbow touches the outside of the right knee. Rotate back toward center, rise up, bring the left leg even with the right, and then repeat the exercise, leading with the left leg. Perform over a distance of 20-30 yards (Hedrick 2000).

CHAPTER 6

Resistance Exercises

Michael Barnes, MEd, CSCS
Richard Borden, PhD, PT, CSCS
Keith E. Cinea, MA, CSCS
Brian Newman, MS, CSCS

Olympic Style Lifts and their Variations

With the power snatch and power clean descriptions, it should be noted that a broad overview of an effective teaching progression is used, but should not be considered the only or the best way to teach these exercises. An NSCA certified strength and conditioning coach with experience should supervise these lifts.

Hang Snatch

Grip Measurement

To determine the grip width for the snatch, measure the distance from the outside of a closed fist to the opposite shoulder. Have the lifter grip the barbell at the measured width.

Starting Position

The power snatch can be effectively taught from a top-down approach. In the starting position, the bar is grasped with a snatch grip. The lifter stands in an upright position, with the chest held high, the wrists slightly flexed, and the elbows fully extended and slightly rotated out from the body. The knees are fully extended, and the neck is in a neutral position, with the lifter looking straight ahead. The bar rests comfortably on the thighs, at the crease of the hip joint.

High Chest Position

The bar is lowered to a mechanically correct position for the athlete to successfully accomplish the power snatch. This position is sometimes referred to as the high-chest position. While maintaining the high-chest position, the knees are flexed to about 15 to 20 degrees. The trunk is angled to about 5 to 10 degrees, and the bar rests on the crease of the hip join. The wrists are flexed, and the elbows are straight and rotated outward. The neck is in a neutral position, and the lifter looks straight ahead.

Power Shrug or Body Fully Extended

From the high-chest position, the body is fully extended. The lifter looks straight ahead, with the wrists flexed, and the elbows rotated outward. The knees are fully extended. The chest is held up, and the shoulders are elevated in the shrug. The important point is that the bar is elevated as high as possible without bending the elbows. The purpose of the high chest-to-full extension is to teach the acceleration of the bar with the large muscles of the lower extremity, hips, and back, before the arms come into play.

The Catch

From the full-extension position, the lifter can pull to the catch overhead. The bar is kept close to the body throughout the movement. When the bar is received overhead, the arms are fully extended. The bar should be over the feet to ensure balance.

Transition from the Knee to High Chest

The next movement is considered the most difficult to master for the lifter. It is called the transition from the knee to the high chest. What makes this movement difficult is pulling from the knees to the high chest, while keeping the knees slightly bent to arrive at the high chest. The events are performed in the following three-step sequence: #1) The lifter, in the high-chest position with the knees still flexed, lowers the bar down the legs to level of the knees. It is important to reach the level of the knees, as this is the position that compromises the mechanics of the lift the most. #2) With the back flat or slightly arched, the lifter reaches the level of the knees, and then, keeping the knees slightly flexed, pulls the bar to the high chest position. #3) From the high-chest position, the lifter executes the lift as previously described. It is important to keep the knees flexed throughout the transition. If the knees straightened out during the transition, the lifter will not have the ability to jump or extend.

Power Snatch

The next series of movements involves teaching the pull from the floor with the thigh brush. The lifter starts from the high-chest position, lowers the bar to the knee position, and then lowers the bar to the floor position by bending at the knees. It is important to note that the lifter should not lower the bar from the knees with the back. This part of the lift must be done with the legs, so that that bar remains as close to the body's center of gravity as possible.

From the floor position, the lifter extends the legs so that the angle of the body to the floor remains constant, and the chest and hips move at the same rate of speed. Once the bar is at the level of the knees, the lifter moves through the transition period to the high chest. From the high chest, the lifter fully extends to power-snatch final position.

Power Clean

The teaching/learning progression for the power clean is basically the same as for the power snatch. Once this progression is thoroughly understood, comparisons between the two lifts are much clearer. It may be of interest to know that many experienced coaches prefer to teach the power snatch before the power clean.

Hang Clean

Starting Position

The power clean can be effectively taught from a top-down approach as well. In the starting position, the bar is grasped with a clean grip, which is slightly outside the shoulders. The lifter stands in an upright position, with the chest held high, the wrists slightly flexed, and the elbows fully extended and slightly rotated out from the body. The knees are fully extended, and the neck is in a neutral position, with the lifter looking straight ahead. The bar rests comfortably on the thighs at the level of the crease of the hip joint.

High-Chest Position

The bar is lowered to a mechanically correct position for the athlete to successfully accomplish the power clean. This position is sometime referred to as the high-chest position. In this position, the knees are flexed to about 15 to 20 degrees, while the high-chest position is maintained. The trunk is angled to about 5 to 10 degrees, and the bar rests on the crease of the hip joint. The wrists are flexed, and the elbows are straight and rotated outward. The neck is in a neutral position, and the lifter looks straight ahead.

Power Shrug or Body Fully Extended

From the high-chest position, the body is fully extended. The lifter looks straight ahead, with the wrists flexed, and the elbows rotated outward. The knees are fully extended. The chest is held up, and the shoulders are elevated in the shrug. The important point is that the bar is elevated as high as possible without bending the elbows. The purpose of the high chest-to-full extension is to teach the acceleration of the bar with the large muscles of the lower extremity, hips, and back, before the arms come into play.

The Catch

From the full-extension position, the lifter can pull to the catch at the shoulders. The bar is kept close to the body throughout the movement. When the bar is received at the shoulders, the elbows are fully flexed. The bar should be over the feet to ensure balance.

Transition from the Knee to High Chest

The next movement is considered the most difficult to master for the lifter. It is called the transition from the knee to the high chest. What makes this movement difficult is the action involved in pulling from the knees to the high chest, while keeping the knees slightly bent to arrive at the high chest. The sequence of events is as follows: #1) The lifter, in the high-chest position with the knees still flexed, lowers the bar down the legs to level of the knees. It is important to reach the level of the knees, since this is the position that compromises the mechanics of the lift the most. #2) With the back flat or slightly arched, the lifter reaches the level of the knees, and then, keeping the knees slightly flexed, pulls the bar to the high-chest position. #3) From the high-chest position, the lifter executes the lift as previously described. It is important to keep the knees flexed throughout the transition. If the knees straightened out during the transition, the lifter will not have the ability to jump or extend.

Power Clean

The next series of movements involves teaching the pull from the floor with the thigh brush. The lifter starts from the high-chest position, lowers the bar to the knee position, and then lowers the bar to the floor position by bending the knees. It is important to note that the lifter does not lower the bar from the knees with the back. This part of the lift must be done with the legs, so that the bar remains as close to the body's center of gravity as possible.

From the floor position, the lifter extends the legs, so that the angle of the body to the floor remains constant, and the chest and hips move at the same rate of speed. Once the bar is at the level of the knees, the lifter moves through the transition period to the high chest. From the high chest, the lifter fully extends to power-clean, final position.

Push Jerk

The push jerk is performed from a standing position, with the purpose to develop the shoulders and increase an athlete's power. In the starting position, the bar is held slightly wider than shoulder width in front of the shoulders. Bending at the knees and hips performs a counter movement to initiate the repetition. Once the counter movement occurs, the athlete accelerates the weight directly overhead in one movement. The athlete needs to be sure to pull the head back as the bar passes in front of the head.

Split Jerk

The split jerk is performed from a standing position, with the purpose to develop the shoulders and increase an athlete's power. A splitting of the feet defines this movement from the push jerk.

The starting position is the same as for the push jerk. Again, the counter movement is performed by bending at the knees and hips. Once the counter movement occurs, the athlete accelerates the weight directly overhead in one movement, splitting the feet forward and back.

Barbell and Dumbell Exercises

Barbell Bench Press

The barbell bench press is performed on a flat bench with a spotter. The barbell is grasped wider than shoulder width, with a pronated, closed grip. Both feet should be flat on the floor, and the back should be flat on the bench. With the assistance of the spotter, the bar is unracked and brought over the lifter's shoulders. The bar is then lowered to the chest. The athlete should not bounce or drop the weight.

Keeping the feet on the floor and the back flat on the bench, the athlete pushes the bar back up, slightly toward the head. When the arms are fully extended, the bar should be above the shoulders. The prime mover in this exercise is the pectoralis major. This exercise is useful in chest development.

Dumbbell Bench Press

The dumbbell bench press is performed from a supine position on the bench. The athlete starts the exercise with the dumbbells on the thighs, in a seated position. While laying back into the supine position, the athlete brings the dumbbells up to chest level. The athlete should keep the dumbbells close to the chest all the way into the supine position. This movement should be spotted.

Once in the supine position, the dumbbells are held in a pronated grip, beside the chest. Keeping the feet flat on the floor and the back flat on the bench, the athlete pushes the dumbbells up toward the ceiling, bringing them together at the top of the movement. The weights should not bang together. This movement should be performed under control.

The athlete then lowers the weights back to the starting position beside the chest before beginning the next repetition. The spotter should spot this exercise as close to the weight as possible. This exercise should not be spotted at the elbows, because such an approach could result in an injury if the lift fails.

When the exercise is completed, the athlete places the weights on the chest and sits up. The prime mover for this exercise is the pectoralis major, with assistance from the shoulders and triceps.

Incline Bench Press

The incline bench press is performed in a supine position on an incline bench. The athlete grasps the barbell with a slightly wider than shoulder-width grip. To begin the exercise, the weight is unracked and set above the shoulders. While maintaining the normal curves of the back, the athlete lowers the weight to the chest. The athlete should avoid bouncing the weight off the chest, pushing the weight straight back up, using the chest muscles. The prime mover for this exercise is the pectoralis major. This exercise is used for chest development. The spotter should be positioned behind the lifter, where they can assist in racking and unracking the weight, along with spotting the exercise for missed repetitions.

Dumbbell Incline Bench Press

The dumbbell incline bench press is performed on an incline bench in the supine position. This exercise is started in the same manner as the dumbbell bench press. While sitting back, the athlete keeps the weights close to the chest. This can be aided by lifting the weights up with the legs to the chest. From the incline-seated position, the athlete holds the weights outside and slightly above the chest. The athlete pushes the weights toward the ceiling, while bringing them together at the top of the movement until the elbows reach full extension. This is a controlled movement; the weights should not bang together at the top of the movement. The athlete then lowers the weights back to the starting position beside the chest, before beginning the next repetition. The spotter should spot the exercise as close to the dumbbells as possible, and assist the lifter into and out of the supine position. The prime mover for this exercise is the pectoralis major.

Push Press

The push press is performed from a standing position. The purpose of this exercise is to develop the shoulders and increase an athlete's power. In the starting position, the bar is held slightly outside and in front of shoulders. A counter movement is performed by bending at the knees and hips. Once the counter movement occurs, the athlete accelerates the weight overhead. This is the push segment of the movement. The press is performed by pressing with the shoulders, which leaves the elbows extended and the weight overhead. The athlete needs to pull the head back as the bar passes in front of the head.

Dumbbell Lateral Raise

The dumbbell lateral raise is performed in the standing position. The dumbbells are held in a neutral position in front of the body, with a slight bend in the elbows. Abduction occurs at the shoulder joint, and the dumbbells are raised in a controlled manner to shoulder level. The prime mover is the medial deltoid, with the trapezius assisting. This exercise is useful for injury prevention.

Dumbbell Bent-Over Lateral Raise

The dumbbell bent-over lateral raise is performed from the standing position, with hip flexion to about 90 degrees. The dumbbells are held in a neutral grip, with the arms extended below the chest. The abdominals are contracted to assist in spine stabilization. With a slight bend in the elbows, the athlete lifts the weights to the side until they reach shoulder level. The dumbbells are then slowly returned to the starting position. The prime movers for this exercise are the posterior deltoid, the trapezius, and the rhomboids.

Dumbbell Upright Row

The dumbbell upright row is executed in the standing position, with a pronated grip. The athlete's torso is held in a neutral and upright position throughout this movement. In the starting position, the dumbbells lightly touch against the thighs, the elbows are fully extended, and the shoulders are depressed. The movement is initiated by flexion at the elbows and abduction and elevation at the shoulder. A full range of motion is reached when the hands are at shoulder level. The prime movers are the medial deltoids and the upper trapezius. The biceps brachii assist.

Barbell Upright Row

With slight variations, the same mechanics apply to the barbell upright row as for the dumbbell upright row. A closed pronated grip is used for this exercise. The main objectives for the movements involved in this exercise are shoulder development and injury prevention.

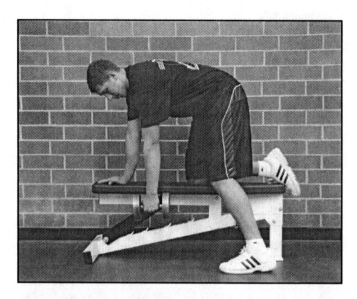

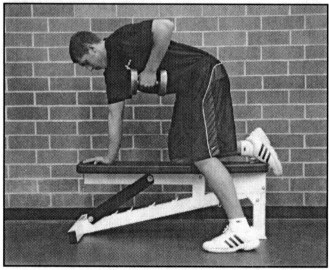

Single-Arm Dumbbell Rows

The single-arm dumbbell row is performed with the hips flexed to 90 degrees. The dumbbell is held in a neutral position, with the arm extended below the shoulder, and the opposite hand and knee on the bench. While maintaining a flat back, the athlete raises the dumbbell to the lower ribs. The elbow is kept beside the body, preventing shoulder abduction. The prime movers in this exercise are the latisimus dorsi and the trapezius. The main objective of this exercise is development of the back musculature.

Lat Pull Down

The pull down exercise is performed in a seated position on a pull down machine. From a standing position, the bar is gripped with a closed, pronated, wider-than-shoulder-width grip. The athlete sits down with the thighs under the pads, and the arms extended overhead holding the bar. While maintaining a neutral spine, the athlete adducts the shoulders and flexes the elbows to lower the bar. The bar is brought down in front of the head to chest level. The althete should not lean back to initiate the movement, or gain an advantage. The weight is then lowered as the arms return to the starting position, extended over the head. The prime mover in this exercise is the latisimus dorsi, with assistance from the biceps brachii.

Back Squat

The back squat is performed in a standing position inside a squat rack. Using a closed, pronated grip, the athlete places the barbell on the back, on top of the scapula. The athlete must not place the bar on the back of the neck. The athlete's feet should be slightly more than shoulder-width apart, with the toes pointed forward or slightly outward. The athlete should keep the abdominals tight to assist in stabilizing the spine.

The athlete squats down to a parallel position, while maintaining an upright torso. The individual should be sure that the feet track with the toes and do not extend horizontally beyond the toes. The athlete extends the knees and hips to raise the body back up to the starting position. The individual should not bounce out of the bottom position. The hips and shoulders should rise at the same speed. The major muscles used during this exercise are the gluteals, quadriceps, and hamstrings. This exercise is used for lower-body development.

Back Squat Spot

A spotter should be used to help rack and unrack the weights. When spotting the back squat, the spotter should stand behind the lifter, and follow the lifter through the complete range of motion. To assist, the hands are in a ready position, and the spotter helps the lifter if needed.

Front Squat

The front squat starts in a standing position in a squat rack. The barbell is griped in a closed, pronated grip. The shoulder joint should be flexed so that the arms are parallel to the ground, with the elbows up. The feet should be slightly more than shoulder-width apart, pointing forward or slightly outward. The athlete maintains a neutral spine, keeping the abdominals tight to stabilize the spine. The lifter squats down, while maintaining an upright posture, until the thighs are parallel to the ground. Without bouncing, the athlete extends back up to the starting position. The major muscles used during this exercise are the gluteals, quadriceps, and hamstrings. This exercise is also used for lower-body development.

Front Squat Spot

A spotter should be used to help rack and unrack the weights. The spotter should stand behind the lifter, and follow the lifter through the complete range of motion. The spotter's hands are in a ready position, in order to help if needed.

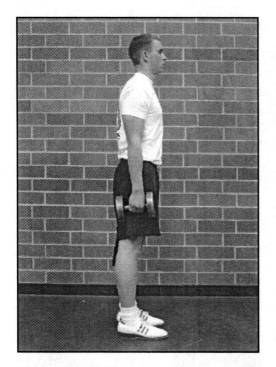

Front Lunge

The front lunge is performed with the dumbbells held in a neutral grip on the outside of the thighs. The abdominals are held tight to assist in spine stabilization. The athlete takes a larger than normal step forward and lowers the body until the thigh of the front leg is parallel to the ground. The athlete should be sure the knee does not go horizontally further than the toes, and that the back knee does not touch the ground. The lifter returns to the starting position by pushing off with the front leg. An upright torso should be maintained throughout the entire exercise. The prime movers for this exercise are the gluteals, hamstrings, and quadriceps. This exercise is useful in lower-body development.

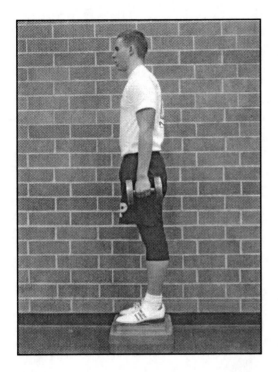 

Reverse Lunge

The reverse lunge can be performed with or without a box. It is started from a standing position, with the dumbbells held in a neutral grip. While maintaining an upright position, the athlete steps back and lowers the body. The athlete should be sure that the knee of the front leg does not travel past the toes. The lifter returns to the starting position by using the front leg to lift the body, while maintaining the upright torso position. The prime movers in this exercise are the gluteals, quadriceps, and hamstrings.

Lateral Lunge

The lateral lunge is performed in the standing position. An effort should be made to ensure that sufficient room exists for the athlete to move laterally. The dumbbells are griped with a neutral grip in front of the body. Keeping the abdominals tight, the athlete takes a step to the side with the toes pointing diagonally. Flexing the knee and the hip, the athlete lowers the body to a parallel position, while keeping the head and chest up. The athlete needs to make sure the knee tracks with the foot, and does not extend horizontally beyond the toes. The lifter pushes back up to the starting position, while maintaining the torso and head upright. The hips and shoulders should raise at the same rate. The exercise should be repeated to the other side. This exercise works the gluteals, quadriceps, hamstrings, and groin muscles. It is useful for lower-body development and injury prevention.

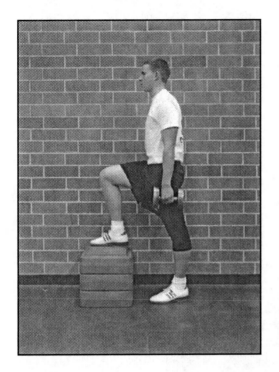 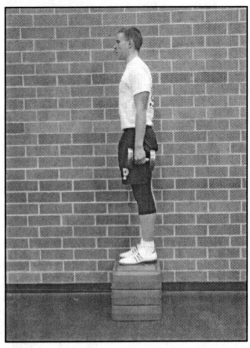

Step Ups

The step up is performed from a standing position, with a step height between 12 to 18 inches. This height should create a ninety-degree angle at the knee. With the dumbbells held in a neutral position on the sides of the body, the athlete places one foot on top of the step. While maintaining an upright torso, the athlete steps up, using the leg on the step. The athlete should avoid an excessive push with the rear foot. The lifter should slowly return to the starting position, while maintaining the torso upright. The prime movers for this exercise are the gluteals, hamstrings, and quadriceps. This exercise develops the lower body.

Dumbbell Bicep Curl

The dumbbell bicep curl is performed in the standing position. The athlete holds the dumbbells in a neutral grip, with the palms facing inward. The torso is constantly kept in an upright position. The lifter should not produce momentum by swinging the torso. The movement is initiated by flexion at the elbow and completed through a full range of motion. The prime movers in this exercise are the biceps group. Variations can include supination (rotating the palms up).

Tricep Extension

The tricep extension is performed from a standing position on a high-pulley cable machine. The rope is gripped with a closed, neutral, shoulder-width grip. In the starting position, the elbows are brought to the sides with the ropes in front of the chest. While maintaining an upright position, the athlete extends the elbow joints, pulling the ropes down until full extension is reached. The ropes are then returned to the staring position by flexion at the elbow before beginning the next repetition. This exercise can also be performed with a straight bar. The prime mover for this exercise is the triceps brachii.

Abdominal Exercises

Crunch

The crunch is performed with the feet flat on the floor, the low back pressed into the floor, and the hands beside the head. If the hands are placed behind the head, the athlete should not interlace the fingers, in order to help prevent pulling on the head. The athlete contracts the abdominal muscles, bringing the chest toward the thighs and the scapula off the ground, before returning back to the starting position. This exercise can also be performed with the arms at the sides, trying to touch the ankles on each repetition. Both of these exercises work the rectus abdominis muscles.

Trunk Rotation

From a supine position with the hands beside the head, the athlete flexes the trunk. While flexing the trunk, the athlete rotates the right shoulder toward the left knee. Slowly, the athlete returns to the starting position and repeats the exercise to the opposite side. This exercise works the oblique muscles.

Leg Raises

To perform leg raises, the athlete sits back with the spine in a neutral position, and the legs extended out in front. The upper body leans backwards, with some body weight supported by the arms. Keeping the legs extended, but the ankles flexed, the athlete brings the legs up to about shoulder level. The legs are lowered back down to just above the ground, and the exercise is repeated. This exercise builds pelvic stability and works the hip flexors.

CHAPTER 7

Plyometrics

Patrick McHenry, MA, CSCS

Plyometrics is a form of jump training that Russian track athletes have used since the early 1960's when Dr. Yuri Verhshanski first developed it for his triple jumpers. It is based on the concept of the stretch-shortening cycle, which states that if a muscle is forcibly stretched, it will cause a greater concentric contraction than if the muscle had not been stretched.

Fred Wilt is credited with introducing plyometrics to the United States at a track clinic in the 1970's. Since its introduction to the United States, numerous studies have been conducted all over the world that have documented its benefits. Plyometric training is referred to by many different names, including shock training, shock method, bounding, jump training, and powermetrics, a term which is growing in popularity with the scientific community.

Plyometrics, like any other training system, has its detractors. For example, plyometrics can result in negative consequences (e.g., cause the exerciser to be injured) if not properly taught and implemented into a periodized, scientifically sound workout. With regard to plyometric training, one important point to remember is that jumping is a part of plyometrics, but not all jumps are plyometrics.

Types of Plyometric Drills

Plyometric drills exist for both upper and lower body. When performing plyometrics, a variety of equipment can be used to perform the prescribed drill. Regardless of which equipment is used for plyometric training, however, the athlete should strictly adhere to all safety considerations (which are discussed later in this chapter), and always keep in mind that quality is more important then quantity when performing plyometric training.

The key factor when executing a plyometric exercise is the stretch-shortening cycle. The stretch-shortening cycle occurs when a muscle is eccentrically contracted, followed immediately by a concentric contraction. The rate and magnitude of the stretch is detected by the muscle spindle, which innervates a motor neuron in the spinal column. This motor neuron then causes a more powerful contraction in the stretched muscle.

The aforementioned attribute is the safety mechanism within the muscles that protects it from over-stretching. To a point, the faster the pre-stretch, the more powerful the contraction is. Keep in mind, however, that if the athlete does not get the quick eccentric contraction that is immediately followed by the concentric contraction with a short amortization phase (the transition between the eccentric and concentric phases), then the athlete is performing basic jumps or throws, not true plyometric exercises. The following lists present examples of plyometric exercises for the upper body and lower body, respectively.

Upper body:

- Chest pass
- Push up (on/off boxes or ground, with medicine balls)
- Throws with medicine balls

Lower body:

- Box jumps
- Shock jumps
- In-place jumps
- Bounding
- Hops

Program Design

To ensure that the program will maximize results while minimizing injuries, the coach needs to first make sure that the athletes are in shape. In this regard, many different guidelines could be followed. For example, the NSCA recommends that athletes be able to free weight squat 1 1/2-2 1/2 times their body weight before starting lower-body plyometrics. For upper-body plyometrics, the ability to do five handclap push-ups or a body-weight bench press is recommended for athletes over 90 kg. The ability to bench press 1 1/2 times their body weight is recommended for those athletes under 90 kg, before starting an upper-body plyometric program (Wathen, 1993). Keep in mind that the aforementioned are only guidelines. It is the coach's responsibility for and insight into their athletes that should dictate what exercises should be employed and when. Furthermore, numerous pre-plyometric or lead-up exercises exist that a coach can use to get their athletes ready for a true plyometric program.

☐ Individual Session

For each session, the coach should follow a typical training session that includes a warm-up, training session, and cool-down (Allerheiligen, 1995). The warm-up should include both general stretching and sports-specific dynamic drills that can vary from sport-to-sport or session-to-session. The other factors that are involved in designing a program for each individual session include frequency, volume, intensity/ type of exercise, and progression.

☐ Frequency

Frequency refers to the number of times the athlete should perform the plyometric routine during the week. Depending upon the sport, it is a general rule of thumb to have 1-2 sessions per week for athletes who are in season, with 24-48 hours rest between the last plyometric session and the competitive event. If the athlete is out of season, then plyometrics should be performed 2-3 times a week, depending on the lifting routine and the particular phase of training the athlete is in.

☐ Volume

Volume is the number of contacts the athlete has with the ground. This factor is based on the athlete's ability level and time of season. Just because an athlete is out of season does not mean the individual should perform high-level plyometrics, especially novice athletes. In this regard, the following guidelines (see chart 7-1) are appropriate: 80-100 contacts/session for beginners; 100-120 contacts/session for intermediate athletes; and 120-140 contacts/session for advanced athletes (Baechle & Earle, 2000). The coach should also remember that an inverse relationship exists between volume and intensity. If the drill is conducted at a high-intensity level, the volume should be low.

☐ Intensity

Intensity refers to the stress put on the individual's musculoskeletal system during the exercise, not the effort put forth by the athlete. Low-level or pre-plyometric exercises can be incorporated into the program more often, and can be performed throughout the year. High intensity exercises need to be performed more in the pre-/off-season, with careful monitoring of contact times. Other factors that will influence the intensity level of plyometric training include the types of contact (one foot/two feet), the direction of the jump (vertical/horizontal), and the height of the box, if performing depth jumps.

Chart 7-1. Recommended intensity guidelines for athletes of different ability/experience levels.

Season	Beginning	Intermediate	Advanced	Intensity
Off -season	60-100	100-150	120-200	Low-moderate
Preseason	100-150	50-300	150-450	Moderate-high
In-season	Sport specific	Sport specific	Sport specific	Moderate
Championship	Recovery	Recovery	Recovery	

Reprinted, by permission, from D.A. Chu, 1998, Jumping into plyometrics, 2nd ed. (Champaign, IL: Human Kinetics), 29.

Definitions of Movements

☐ *Jump:* A linear movement that ends with a 2-foot landing. Can be performed in place (tuck, pike, split) or linear (standing long jump, triple jump).

☐ *Hop:* A movement that starts and ends with 1-or 2-foot landing on the same foot or both feet.

☐ *Bound:* A movement where the athlete jumps from one foot and lands on the other.

☐ *Shock:* A depth jump or box jump. The athlete steps off a box, lands on the ground, and jumps as quickly as possible. The force involved in landing puts great stress on the joints, muscles, and connective tissue. As such, this type of plyometric exercise should be performed only by those individuals who are highly conditioned. It is an exercise that should involve low repetitions, and should be performed minimally throughout the training cycle.

Progression

Progression is the order the exercises are performed. Proper progression for lower body exercises may consist of jump rope, followed by 2-foot jumps in place. As the athlete becomes more proficient on the take-off and landing, the individual can begin performing 2-foot jumps with a horizontal component, or jumps-in-place on one foot. This sequence would be followed by bounding and end with box jumps or depth jumps.

When deciding the height of the boxes to use, a simple test can be used. According to Lord & Campagna, 1997, the first step, in this regard, is to find the athlete's vertical jump height. Next, athletes should be instructed to perform jumps off

Chart 7-2. Suggested plyometric exercises, depending on drill type and intensity level.

Drill Type	Low Intensity	Medium Intensity	High Intensity	Shock
In-place	• Ankle bounce • Tuck jump • Split jump • Lateral jump • Ice skater	• Cycle jump • Drop jump • Lateral hop	• Hops	• Depth drop
Short response < or = 10 Repetitions or < 30 meters	• Standing long jump	• Three continuous standing long jumps • Standing triple jump • Single hurdle jump • Crossover lateral bound	• Five continuous standing long jumps • Double leg box jumps • 5-10 hurdle rebound jumps	• Continuous hurdle hops • Box bounds
Long response > or = 10 Repetitions or > 30 meters	• Leaps	• 10 + Hops	• Speed bounds • Alternate leg bounds • Single leg bounds	
Upper body	• Two handed overhead forward throw • Chest pass • Clapping push-up • Medicine ball push-up	• Overhead backwards throw • Underhand forward throw • Drop push-ups	• Drop rebound push-ups	• One-arm push-ups
	Beginner	Intermediate	Advanced	

a box, trying to touch their original vertical height. If the athlete cannot reach their original vertical jump, then the box is too high and will not enable the individual to achieve the results needed.

For the upper body, the athlete's progression could start with some push-ups, that could lead into chest passes with a medicine ball, followed by push-ups on and off boxes, and finishing with drop push-ups. If the box push-ups cannot be performed on the toes, the athlete should start out on the knees, then progress to the toes.

Whether upper or lower body, the coach needs to make sure correct technique is emphasized at all times, and stress that quality is more important then quantity. These progressions may take a month or longer, depending on the athlete's physical attributes (i.e., balance, strength, coordination). The athlete should be closely monitored by the coach so the athlete does not try to do too much, too soon.

Safety

Injured athletes are virtually of no use—to their coach, their teammates, or themselves. In fact, athletes who injures themselves can jeopardize everything for which their strength coach has worked. With regard to safety, several factors should be addressed. Along with the design of the plyometrics program, other safety factors include the age/athletic ability of the individual, the area that the drills are performed in, footwear, and technique.

Age/athletic ability must be considered because the coach may have an athlete who is a senior in high school, yet has only been training for three months versus a sophomore who has been training for three years. Obviously, the younger athlete is more experienced and could handle more than the older athlete whose training age is different. Training programs need to reflect the differences in each athlete's ability. This objective can be accomplished by exercising the athletes in separate sessions, or by employing separate stations for performing different exercises.

The area in which the exercises are performed must also be evaluated when designing the plyometrics workout. The strength coach needs to make sure that his athletes are not jumping and landing on hard surfaces, or doing exercises in an area that is too forgiving, thereby prohibiting the athlete from exploding off it. The ideal surface is an aerobic dance floor, or one that has some give to it. Wrestling mats, wood floors, most grass surfaces, tracks, or any other surface that has give, yet still maintains a stable enough surface for rebounding, make a suitable surface. Thick gymnastic mats, concrete, and even some old astro-turf surfaces are too hard, a factor that can lead to stress fractures or overuse injuries.

Other areas such as sand or water do not allow the athlete to push off. As a result, the athlete is not performing a true plyometric exercise. These surfaces are not always bad, however. There may be times when the coach wants to do some lead-up exercises or make the workout an easy training session, so they will utilize one of these areas to allow the athlete to get in a light workout.

Footwear is a factor because it can cause problems with ankle stability when exercising (Siff & Verkhoshansky, 2000). Some of the running shoes that are currently popular are too narrow at the bottom, and can cause an athlete to turn an ankle if the landing is not just right. With regard to plyometric training, wear a basketball, cross-trainer, or court shoe that has proper cushioning, a sturdy side, and a stable base to prevent any twisting of the ankle.

Technique on the take off and landing is probably one of the most important, yet often-ignored, factors in teaching plyometrics. Research has shown the correct use of the arms can contribute 10% or more to the vertical jump (Gambetta, 1987). The short, upward movement of the arms used on take off, or blocking as it is sometimes referred to, must be taught and reinforced at all times (O'Shea, 2000). To execute correct blocking with the arms, the elbows need to be flexed at approximately 90 degrees, with the hands near the hips. Then, the athlete should thrust their hands upward, so the hands end just in front of their face. The movement should be from the shoulders, while maintaining flexion at the elbows throughout the complete upward movement. Some common mistakes in this regard include flexing and extending at the elbow so there is no motion from the shoulders, bringing the hands behind the hips as if winding up the arms, and using the arms for balance by having them abducted at the shoulder.

The landing should focus on proper foot placement, flexion at the ankle, knee, and hip, and the amount of force produced when the feet hit the ground. According to Komi and Bosco (1978), foot placement should be about shoulder-width apart, with maximum hip flexion at 130 degrees, knee flexion at 110 degrees, and the heels not touching the ground. The upper body should not flex at the waist, and the back must maintain its normal curvature. If the athlete lands too hard, they may make a "thump" or "slapping" sound. This sound is an indication the athlete is landing incorrectly. Remember, the force with which the athlete hits the ground is going through their body and can lead to injuries. When a proper plyometric jump is executed, the coach should barely be able to hear the athlete touch the ground.

CHAPTER 8

Speed Development

Ian Jeffreys, MSc, CSCS, *D

Because speed is perceived by many coaches as the most important aspect of athletic performance, hence the importance placed on it in testing and selection policies. Once thought of as a genetically determined factor, speed is generally now acknowledged as a factor that can be improved by a scientifically designed program.

In setting up a program to develop speed, it should be noted that the 100-meter sprint model does not necessarily provide an ideal model on which to base a sport-specific speed model. Distances in sport tend to be shorter, and movements are multi-lateral. Hence, the coach needs to break down the specific speed and agility requirements of the sport prior to constructing the speed and agility program.

Speed and agility training should not be viewed in isolation. Effective speed-and-agility performance is based upon appropriate conditioning in a number of areas. Essentially, speed and agility are dependent on explosive force, thus all training methods that impact this aspect of performance need to be addressed. A speed athlete needs appropriate levels of strength and power development, flexibility, body composition, and speed endurance.

Determinants of Speed

The following characteristics affect an individual's running speed:

- *Muscle factors:* Relating to muscle-related properties, including fiber-type distribution, degree of development, and contraction characteristics.
- *Skill factors:* Essentially neuromuscular coordination relating to the ability to produce powerful, coordinated muscle actions.
- *Elastic Factors:* Relating to the body's ability to store energy in the musculotendinous unit and utilize it on subsequent concentric contractions.
- *Anatomical factors:* Relating to muscle alignment during movement, muscle insertion points, lever lengths, and body composition.

Although a number of these factors cannot be controlled, many are capable of adaptation. What is clear is the role of the neuromuscular system, and hence the skilled nature of speed. Speed is a motor skill, and thus teachable and trainable. Just as for any other attribute, this skill needs to be taught and practiced if effective motor programs are to be developed. High school programs have a vital role in ensuring that all athletes develop efficient and effective running styles to maximize their performance.

Aspects of Speed

Running speed is directly related to the relationship between stride length and stride rate. Stride length is affected by the ground-reaction forces developed during running, and is thus directly related to the speed-strength characteristics of the leg and hip musculature. Stride rate is more difficult to improve, but can be through the use of sprint drills and sprint-assisted methods.

In most sports, the key factor in linear speed is not the top speed achieved, but the ability to accelerate. Acceleration refers to the rate of change of velocity over time. Thus, athletes need to be able to reach peak or optimal velocity in as short a time period as possible.

It is also possible to identify two aspects of acceleration: pure acceleration (0-10 meters) and transition acceleration (11-30 meters). Some sports require the ability to move from stationary positions, while others require the ability to move from rolling-type starts. Speed programs should ensure that the sport-specific requirements of acceleration are met.

Phases of the Sprint Action

Three phases of the sprint action can be identified—the drive, recovery, and support:

The Drive Phase

This phase occurs predominantly during late support. It is important to remember that the power for sprinting comes from the forces directed into the ground. Thus the aim of this phase is to maximize the push off from the ground. In this part of the sprint action, forces are distally phased, with forces generated first at the hip, then the knee, and finally the ankle joint.

The Recovery Phase

This aspect of the sprint action follows the drive phase, and is characterized by a closing of the knee joint, which reduces the lever arm of the leg, thereby providing a shorter lever for a faster motion. The leg then cycles through and extends in preparation for touchdown. This phase can be divided into early, middle, and late recovery.

The Support Phase

During this phase, the foot makes contact with the ground. At this point, the calf musculature absorbs energy, which can then be utilized in the drive phase via the stretch-shortening cycle.

Running Mechanics

Two basic mechanical models can be identified for linear speed, relating to acceleration and maximum running speed—the acceleration model and the maximum-speed model. For both models coaching emphasis should be on the following three areas: body alignment, arm action, and leg action.

The Acceleration Model

- *Body alignment.* During this phase, the body has a pronounced forward lean. This lean should ideally be generated via a straight body, and not by any excessive flexion in the back. The aim is to generate a straight line from head to toe.

- *Arm action.* Arm action through all phases should occur at the shoulder. During this phase, arm action is powerful, and involves a greater range of motion than in the maximum-speed model. Hand position, to an extent, is a matter of preference, with either an open hand or a loosely cupped action being suitable. At no time should the hands be clenched or any tension developed.

- *Leg action.* Similarly, knee action involves an exaggerated knee lift, with the objective being to generate an effective drive and an applied ground force. In this phase, ground contact time is at its greatest, allowing for greater ground force to be applied. After the first two strides, foot contact will occur in front of the center of gravity, with this distance subsequently decreasing as speed increases.

The Maximum-Speed Model

This mechanical model is normally divided into two actions—the stride and the lift. Essentially, the two actions are similar, with the lift being seen as the kick at speed.

☐ The stride action

- *Body alignment.* Effective stride action involves a tall running posture; athletes should be encouraged to imagine a balloon pulling them upwards. Athletes should also be instructed to avoid allowing the hips to sink too low. If the hips sink, stride length will be negatively affected.

- *Arm action.* Arm action needs to be powerful but relaxed, emphasizing the backwards arm drive. The arm angle should be approximately 120 degrees behind the body, closing to 30 degrees in front (although maintaining 90 degrees throughout is often quoted, in reality, this factor seldom occurs). The hand should come back just past the hips and brush close to the hips as it moves. In front, the hand will come up to approximately chin level. The hands should be held in the preferred position, with no tension present.

- *Leg action.* Leg action involves a powerful knee lift, followed immediately by a closing of the knee angle, thus reducing the lever arm. The lower leg then extends during late recovery and makes contact with the ground. With a clawing, striking action, the athlete should feel as if they are pulling the ground backwards behind the body. Foot contact should be approximately under the center of gravity to avoid any braking effect. The leg should then actively push into the ground to provide the necessary ground-reaction forces for effective stride-length development.

☐ The Lift Action

This factor essentially involves a kick at speed. The lift action is similar to the stride action, but with a quicker stride rate and arm action (while maintaining range and drive).

These models only apply after the athlete has sprinted approximately 20-30 meters. In fact, for many sports, they are seldom used. Similarly, the running-tall effect can be counter effective, because the high center of gravity can reduce stability, such as in situations where changes of direction are required or contact is likely. Although proper running mechanics should be developed, care must be taken to ensure that appropriate time is allocated to their development, based on their importance to the athlete's specific sport requirements.

The Practice of Speed Development

Speed development programs often vary. Normally, however, most of these programs include the following components: technique development, running at speed, sprint loading, sprint-assisted training, and speed endurance.

Technique Development

One of the key elements of a high school-conditioning program is ensuring that athletes move as efficiently and effectively as possible. Relative to speed, it is essential that an effective sprinting technique be stressed from the first day of the program. Sprinting is a motor skill, one that needs to be developed as such.

Technique drills provide effective tools with which to develop motor skills. A drill essentially breaks down the whole technique and focuses on specific parts of the skill involved. As such, it is essential that drills be chosen that accurately develop an integral part of the sprinting technique, and are not chosen at random or as ends in themselves. At all times during the drills, technique must be stressed. Accordingly, drills should be chosen that help develop each of the key areas identified in sprinting technique, including arm action, posture, and leg action.

Arm-Action Drill

Arm Swings

The objective of this drill is to develop a relaxed and powerful arm action. This drill is a stationary exercise that is done from a standing position. In this drill, the athlete performs a running action with the arms alone.

Key points:

• Arm action occurs at the shoulder joint.

• The shoulders are held low and relaxed.

• The arms swing straight forward, brushing clothing.

• The hands are held relaxed (either open or cupped, but not clenched).

• The elbows should be held at a 90-degree angle at the arm when possible (subsequently, the arms straighten out somewhat, behind the body).

This drill can also be performed in a seated position, and can be developed into a more powerful action. Resistance can be added in the form of bands, dumbbells, etc.

Posture Drills

Acceleration Posture

A key factor in this area is to encourage the athlete to develop an effective forward lean. This lean can assist the athlete in driving forward from a low position, an attribute which is essential for effective acceleration.

Partner Fall

The aim of this drill is to develop a feel for the forward-lean, acceleration position. This drill involves using a partner. In the drill, the athlete is encouraged to fall forward to a position where his partner supports the athlete. This action develops a feel for the low-body position that is required for effective sprinting.

Key points:

- The athlete should keep their body in a straight position.
- The athlete should not raise their hips.
- The head should be held in a neutral position.

Supported Sprint

The aim of this drill is to carry out a full driving, sprinting action, while maintaining a low-body position. The drill is conducted from the same supported position as the partner fall drill. In this drill, the athlete performs a rapid sprinting motion, using arm and leg drive for three seconds.

Key points:

- The body is maintained in a low position.
- A straight body line should be encouraged.
- The athlete should do a full leg drive to the straight position.

Fall Forward and Sprint

The aim of this drill is to develop the "feeling" for maintaining a low-body position when accelerating. The drill is performed from a standing position. In this drill, the athlete falls forward, and then sprints for 5 to 10 meters. The key point that should be emphasized in this situation is the forward body-lean element of acceleration.

Key points:

- The athlete should stay low.
- A full drive from back leg.
- A powerful knee drive.
- Rapid first few strides.
- A rapid and powerful arm action.

Leg Action Drills

Leg actions can be partitioned into stride and lift actions. In turn, these actions can be broken down into key phases for technique-drill development.

Knee Lift

The aim of this drill is to encourage a powerful knee drive. The knee lift drill can be done in place, marching, skipping, or at full speed.

Key points:

- Land using the ball of the foot.
- Push the leg down as the other knee comes up.
- Keep the supporting leg straight.
- Dorsiflex the foot as it lifts off of the ground.
- Encourage light, rapid foot contact.
- Avoid backward body lean.

Devices/equipment, such as mini hurdles, can be utilized to help the athlete develop knee lift. The speed of these drills can be increased to the point where the athlete is performing full-speed efforts. The emphasis should be on avoiding change in technique at differing speeds.

Down and Ups

The aim of this drill is to encourage a light, fast ground contact. A variation of the knee-lift drill, this drill involves having the athlete bring the foot down and back up in a skipping-like action. The emphasis should be on low ground contact time, with the ground effort bouncing the foot up into the high-knee position.

Key points:

- Land using the balls of the feet.
- Push down as the knee comes up.
- Keep the supporting leg straight.
- Dorsiflex the foot as it lifts off of the ground.
- Encourage light, rapid foot contact.

Pawing

The aim of this drill is to develop a powerful, claw-back action at ground contact. In this drill, the athlete flexes the hip, and then simultaneously flexes at the knee and extends at the hip. At that point, the athlete actively paws the ground. The emphasis should be on the athlete pulling the ground underneath the body, thus contributing to ground forces. The pawing foot should aim to land under the center of gravity to maximize the pushing forces and minimize any braking effect. The progression for performing the drill can be to do the drill from a stationary position, to walking, to running, to sprinting.

Key points:

- Hip flexion preceding all other movements.
- Rapid cycling of the leg into an extended position.
- Pawing action at contact.
- Contact on the ball of the foot.
- Ground contact under the center of gravity.

Butt Kickers

The aim of this drill is to develop an active recovery leg cycle. This drill is designed to shorten the lever arm. In this drill, the lower leg swings back to contact the buttocks. The athlete should be encouraged to bring the heel up without it passing behind the body. Imagining a wall behind the body can assist the athlete in bringing the heel straight up. It is essential that the butt-kick part of this drill be performed after a powerful knee lift, because this is what occurs during sprinting.

Key points:

- Hip flexion is performed first.
- The knees are not kept low during the movement.
- Rapid butt-kicking action follows hip flexion.
- Ground contact is on the ball of the foot.
- Appropriate arm action is emphasized.

Bounds

The objective of this drill is to encourage a powerful drive off the ground and to develop the straight-back leg principle. While bounds are essentially a plyometric drill, the aim of this exercise is to encourage the feeling of the straight leg push from behind the body in the acceleration phase. It is essentially high skipping in the air, with a left, right, left, right pattern. While performing the drill, the athlete strives to achieve distance and a straight-back leg.

Key points:

- Propulsion comes from effective ground-reaction forces.
- The back leg is straightened.
- Hang time is emphasized.
- The high knee-lift position is developed.
- A powerful arm action should be utilized.
- Effective and active ground contact is on the balls of the feet.

Quick Feet

The objective of this drill is to encourage a rapid leg turnover (stride rate). In this drill, the athlete attempts to take as many steps as possible in a ten-meter space. Speed ladders can be a useful tool in this drill.

Key points:

- Rapid leg turnover should be emphasized.
- Ground contact should be on the ball of the foot.
- Light, rapid, and powerful ground contact should be encouraged.
- The foot should be dorsiflexed.
- Arm action should be emphasized.

Stick Drill

The objective of this drill is to develop an effective acceleration action of the gradual stride lengthening. In this drill, an adjustable ladder or sticks are placed at an increasing distance between rungs or sticks. The athlete simply accelerates through the ladder. This drill encourages rapid turnover, followed by a gradual lengthening of the stride.

Key points:

- The first strides are rapid.
- While maintaining cadence (stride rate), the stride length should gradually be increased.
- Initial acceleration posture and action should be stressed.
- Light and rapid ground contact on the balls of the feet should be encouraged.
- The foot should be dorsiflexed.

Ground contact needs to be made on the balls of the feet, a factor requiring great strength and stability at the ankle joint. Single-leg ankle flips are just one of a number of drills that can be performed to develop this active ankle action.

Single Leg Ankle Flips

The objective of this drill is to encourage active ground contact via ankle dorsiflexion and subsequent plantar flexion. During this drill a straight leg is maintained, propulsion is provided at the ankle joint. The athlete initially dorsiflexes the ankle, and then plantar flexes it on contact in order to develop force into the ground.

Key points:

- Straight leg position.
- Active dorsiflexion.
- Active ground contact.
- Powerful plantar flexion.

Running at Speed

To develop speed in any program, it is essential that a certain amount of time be devoted to quality speed work. At all times, this effort should involve quality, maximal work, with adequate rest periods. In setting up the speed-development program, it is essential that the exact sport requirements of the athlete are determined. These requirements involve the following three factors: 1) the distance sprinted (this component will determine how much training needs to be devoted to accelerative and maximal speed work; 2) the directional requirements (in most sports, multi-directional movement is more common, and thus the speed program needs to take account of this circumstance); and 3) the initial velocity (some sports require an athlete to start from a stationary position, whereas others require an acceleration of an athlete already in motion). Among the exercises that an athlete can perform to improve speed are stationary starts, acceleration runs, and ins-and-outs.

☐ Stationary starts

Stationary starts are traditional sprints, in which the athlete is required to sprint for a given distance from a stationary start.

☐ Accelerative runs

Accelerative runs are a series of runs/sprints that are done in a series (pattern) where the emphasis is on a gradual acceleration. For example, for a 90-meter sprint, the pattern might initially involve a 30-meter stride, then 30-meters run faster than the first 30 meters, and finally, 30 meters performed fastest of the three elements. This drill is sometimes referred to as gears, because the athlete is encouraged to "go through the gears" during the run. This drill is especially useful for athletes who need to reach maximum speed, since it can be performed without the fatigue of an all-out effort over the accelerative period. This drill is also an ideal exercise for those athletes who need to accelerate off a rolling start.

☐ Ins-and-outs

Ins-and-outs are used to contrast running between maximum and sub-maximum speeds. The patterns of sequences within the ins-and-outs can be changed to accommodate to requirements of a specific sport. The emphasis on "ins" is to achieve maximum acceleration and speed, while the focus on "outs" is to run fast, but relaxed. For example, an in-and-out involving a 60-meter sprint (20 meters in, 20 meters out, 20 meters in) would require the athlete to sprint flat-out for 20 meters, and then run relaxed for the following 20 meters, followed by a further acceleration and maximum effort for the final 20 meters. This sequence allows for the development of acceleration from both a stationary position and a moving speed. The "out" portion of the sprint can also be used to develop the athlete's ability to cruise at a high pace, using a relaxed, sprinting action.

Sprint Loading

This component of speed development is designed to develop highly specific speed strength. It is based on overloading the sprint action to produce more explosive concentric forces. Sprint loading can involve a number of activities, including hill sprinting, sprinting with added weight, and towing. The critical factor, at all times in this form of training, is to ensure that distances and rest periods are appropriate for the athlete's normal sprinting. If a modified action is utilized, it will negate any possible benefits of this type of training.

☐ Hill sprinting

Hill sprinting is a unique type of hill training that need to be differentiated from hill training used to develop speed endurance. This developmental activity should be performed on a low-grade hill (8-10 degrees), and at an appropriate distance, depending on the desired outcomes. Similarly, rest periods should be scheduled to allow for full recovery.

☐ Weight-loaded sprints

In this method of training, resistance in the form of a weighted vest or belt can be added to the athlete's body to provide an additional overload. Again, an appropriate level of resistance should be selected—one that does not alter the athlete's sprint mechanics.

☐ Towing

Towing is possibly the most versatile method of sprint loading. Resistance can be provided by a variety of devices and methods, including sleds, tires, partners, rubber tubing, etc. An appropriate form of resistance should be selected. For example, as a guideline, the athlete's level of speed should not be slowed by more than 10%.

Towing can also allow for contrast training, in which resisted and unresisted sprints are applied during the same sequence. For example, two resisted runs can be followed by one unresisted run, with the pattern repeating for the required number of runs. The contrast during the training can also be provided within a run by releasing the resistance. Table 8-1 illustrates an example of a sprint-loading progression, designed specifically for high-school athletes.

Table 8-1. Sample sprint loading progression for high-school athletes.

Week	Distance	Repetitions	Contrast added
1	10 meters	4	No
2	15 meters	5	No
3	15 meters	5	After sprint 3,5
4	20 meters	6	After sprint 3,5
5	20 meters	6	After sprint 2,4,6
6	20 meters	6	After sprint 2,4,6

The twenty-meter distance provides an overload for the pure accelerative aspect of speed performance. Greater distances should be progressively utilized for athletes who are concerned with longer accelerative performance. At all times quality is the key. This training is aimed at developing speed strength, as opposed to speed endurance.

Sprint-Assisted Training

The objective of sprint-assisted (or overspeed) training is to provide a further overload by allowing the athlete to sprint at speeds that exceed their existing capabilities. This method can develop both stride length and stride rate. Methods of applying sprint-assisted training include downhill sprinting and towing.

As in sprint-resisted training, it is essential that the mechanics of the sprint are not altered during the application. In high-school settings, critical safety factors should always govern the application of overspeed training.

Sprint-assisted training should only be undertaken by athletes who have a strong background in sprint training, and have the necessary technique and speed strength to tolerate this type of training. It should always be placed early in a session, following a thorough warm-up. The initial intensity and volume levels of this type of training should be low, in order to allow the athlete to adapt to this type of training.

□ Downhill sprinting

The effectiveness of this type of training will depend on finding a suitable hill. A 3-degree slope is ideal, with seven degrees being the maximum safe slope. Ideally, a flat area should precede the hill to allow for acceleration to top speed, followed by a 15 to 30-meter downhill section, and then a further flat area for deceleration. Because hills like this are few and far between, common sense needs to prevail. As such, all training sessions should be planned to maximize the effectiveness of available hills.

□ Towing

The application of overspeed training has become easier with the advent of various tubing and pulley equipment, allowing for more varied applications. This equipment also permits the application of overspeed training to sport-specific movements, such as sideways shuffles or back-pedals. The volume and intensity of towing drills used will depend upon both the nature of the athlete and the phase of training. At no time should the pull be so great as to alter the athlete's sprint mechanics. Table 8-2 provides an example of an overspeed training progression for high-school athletes.

Table 8-2. Sample 6-week overspeed training progression for high-school athletes.

Week	Distance	Repetitions	Intensity*
1	15 meters	3	+3%
2	15	3	+5%
3	20	4	+5%
4	20	4	+7%
5	25	5	+7%
6	25	5	+10%

*In this instance, intensity is measured as a percentage of maximal speed, and is gauged by timing the overspeed run and comparing it with the athlete's best time over that distance.

Long-Term Development

It is important to work on a long-term plan for developing speed. Athletes must be introduced to speed training early, since the window of opportunity for speed development closes at a relatively young age. After this period, speed improvements are mainly through enhanced power output. Thus, young athletes need to have the opportunity to enhance movement speed prior to their window of opportunity closing.

In the early stages of development, it is essential that basic sprint mechanics, innervation drills, and a sound strength base are addressed. Only when these foundations are laid, can the other developmental methods, such as sprint loading, sprint-assisted training, etc., be effectively applied.

The Periodization of Speed

The primary speed emphasis should take place in the late pre-competitive periods and competitive periods of a periodized year. However, it is vital that some speed work is performed at all times, even in general preparatory work. Speed is a neuromuscular skill, and the speed pathways have to be constantly stimulated. Not including speed sessions in the athlete's developmental efforts is to neglect these pathways, and can result in less-than-optimum speed development.

Session Organization

Clearly the organization of a developmental session for speed will vary with the setting in which it is delivered. In some instances, it may be a dedicated speed session; in other cases, it may be linked with other variables, such as agility or plyometrics. Furthermore, it may be part of a team's practice, in which a part of the session has been dedicated for speed enhancement. Whatever the situation, it is vital that quality speed work is performed early in the session when the athlete is fresh and is able to work at the required intensity to enhance speed.

For those sessions devoted completely to speed development, the following organizational sequence can be adhered to:

- Active warm-up, to include dynamic flexibility.
- Innervation of neural pathways.
- Technical development.
- Maximum speed work.
- Sprint loading.
- Specific sport drills.
- Speed endurance.

The active warm-up phase should include movements that raise the body's temperature. Drills performed at a low intensity, such as cariocas, provide an ideal way of raising body temperature, while working on mechanics. Dynamic flexibility movements can be added that allow an athlete to move through a range of motion and then work back through it. Lunges provide a good example of a dynamic flexibility movement that can be used effectively in a sprint warm-up.

☐ Innervation of neural pathways

The innervation phase requires rapid movements that have the effect of stimulating the neural pathways required for fast sprinting. This factor develops speed of movement and coordination of movements. Quickfoot and ladder drills are ideal at this time.

☐ Technical development

During the technical development phase, specific sprint drills are emphasized to develop specific aspects of performance. It is important to determine what is to be worked on, and then select the best drills to develop the required performance. These drills also provide a continued warm-up prior to any maximal efforts.

☐ Maximum speed work

Any maximum speed and sprint assisted work is performed in the maximum speed phase. Speed work will vary, depending upon which aspect of speed is being developed (e.g. acceleration or maximum speed). Accordingly, the coach must choose the best exercises to develop that aspect. It is vital to ensure that the athlete is not in a fatigued state when performing any of this type of work. As such, appropriate rest periods need to be used to ensure full recovery between runs. A drop in the athlete's run quality is a sign to terminate this work.

☐ Sprint loading

Sprint loading work, such as resisted sprinting as well as any plyometric drills, should take place following the maximum-speed work phase.

☐ Specific-sport drills

In the specific sport skills phase, sport-specific drills should be employed that encourage the athlete to incorporate the skills developed previously into highly sport-specific movements. Movement patterns, distances, and sport skills are all factors that are considered in this phase.

Speed Endurance

Any speed endurance work needs to be completed at the end of the developmental session, for speed, or as a separate session in itself. This work should address the principal energy systems that are utilized during the sport, and should be as sport-specific as possible. Clearly, not all aspects will be worked on in a single session, and each session should have a specific goal. The aforementioned guidelines provide a logical order of execution that helps ensure optimal effectiveness of each phase.

CHAPTER 9

Agility

Ian Jeffreys, MSc, CSCS, *D
Patrick McHenry, MA, CSCS

Some of the greatest moments in sport reflect the demonstration of agility. Although most coaches know superb agility when they see it, defining it, and thus training it, is more difficult. In essence, agility can be looked at as athleticism, and involves the motor-skill components of power, coordination, explosive changes in direction or speed (acceleration and deceleration), dynamic balance, the ability to maintain coordinated movements under pressure from opposition, and quickness (the ability to read and react quickly and effectively to stimuli). Thus, an agility program needs to involve both reactive work and movement work.

Just as speed can be improved by training, so can agility, although the research on this area is less conclusive. However, agility is a more difficult term to define and measure than is speed. Each sport, and even each playing position, will impose specific agility-based demands on the athlete. Therefore, when designing agility programs, it is essential to deconstruct the movement requirements of particular sports and playing positions, and identify movement skills and patterns required within the sport. Once that objective is accomplished, training programs and drills can be generated to specifically address the movement demands of the sport and the position.

Agility training must not be seen in isolation. It must be part of a multi-faceted program that develops all of the aspects of superior performance. Effective agility is dependent on a sound basis of strength and power development, flexibility, balance, and motor-movement patterns.

Determinants of Agility

Agility can be seen to have a number of fundamental components, that themselves rely on sound underlying physiology and biomechanics. The following factors can affect agility:

Muscle factors

The fiber type distribution, degree of development, nature of innervation, and contraction characteristics can all affect agility.

Skill factors

Neuromuscular co-ordination (both inter-muscular and intra-muscular), relating to the ability to produce powerful, coordinated muscle actions, can affect agility.

Elastic factors

The body's ability to store energy in the musculotendinous unit and utilize it on subsequent concentric contractions can affect agility.

Anatomical factors

Muscle alignment during movement, lever lengths, muscle insertion points, and body mass and composition can all contribute to mechanical efficiency, which, in turn, can affect agility.

Total Agility

Pure agility is extremely difficult to isolate, as its performance is intricately linked with a number of other parameters. In developing total agility, it is important to ensure that the following areas are addressed: balance (both static and dynamic), reaction time (ideally to sport specific stimuli, and multiple stimuli), accelerative ability, deccelerative ability, and body movement control (including visual focus, body movements, and footwork).

Types of Agility

Agility can involve movement of the whole body or of body parts. Similarly, movements can occur predominantly horizontally, predominantly vertically, or as a combination of both. They can also involve changes in level or position, and have a locomotive or acrobatic component. Thus, agility training needs to address the specific requirements of an athlete.

Agility can be termed closed or open. Closed agility refers to movements that are pre-programmed. They are ideal to teach basic movement patterns, but their sport-specific application is limited. Once basic movement patterns have been developed, more open agility drills should be introduced to the program.

Open agility refers to movements that are random. These movements require the athlete to read and react to a stimulus, such as another athlete's movement, and to respond appropriately. Mirror drills and tag activities would fall into this random category. The introduction of more sport-specific stimuli can also help develop reactive ability and hence contribute effectively to quickness development.

Agility can be general or specific, with general agility referring to gross movement such as side shuffling. Specific agility refers to the skill involved in a specific speed or direction.

Areas of Focus

When developing agility, the following areas of focus need to be examined:

The feet

Light ground contact is essential to ensure that maximum ground-contact forces can be applied. Similarly, the dorsiflexed (toe up) position must be stressed at all times. The feet should be placed perpendicular to the direction of movement, with weight on the balls of the feet, not on the toes. When planting the foot to cut, the foot should be placed flat to allow for maximum force generation.

The ankles

As in speed development, effective agility movement depends upon the effective use of the energy generated via the stretch-shorten cycle. Thus, the ankles must be trained to utilize this source. Again, the dorsiflexed position is essential for effective movement.

The linear and lateral muscles

In sprinting, the drive muscles that generate linear motion dominate (quadriceps, glutes and hamstrings). Lateral movement requires an athlete to shuffle, cross step, cut, etc. Emphasis must be placed on the muscles that generate these movements (e.g., hip flexors, adductors, and abductors).

The torso

The hip must be stressed in the performance of agility drills, because quick movement originates here. In addition, effective movement requires a strong and stable base, which is provided by a strong torso musculature. Core stability practice can provide the stable platform from which all other movements can be generated.

The neuromuscular system

The neuromuscular system must be a primary focus of training. This system should be trained to activate the muscles quickly and carry out movements at rapid speeds.

Positive Angles

A cornerstone of effective movement is the ability to read and react to a stimulus and then move efficiently and effectively in response. One of the key areas is putting the body in a position where it can effectively move in any required direction without the need for any other counter movements that may slow total movement. In other words, the body is loaded, and positive angles contribute to this loading. Thus, positive angles need to be generated at the ankle, knee, and hip. The positive angles need to be applied within an effective base of support that provides the stable platform from which effective angles can be applied.

Developing Agility Skills

Basic learning processes apply to agility. Athletes will initially enter the cognitive stage, where movements tend to be jerky, uncoordinated, and require great thought. In this stage, closed-technique drills are paramount. Following the cognitive stage, most athletes will transfer into the motor stage, where the skill is refined. At this point, closed drills are still important, but a range of open movements and sport-specific stimuli need to be introduced. Some athletes will then enter the autonomous phase, where they can produce movement almost automatically. At this stage, open drills, using highly sport-specific movements, are predominate.

Massed Versus Distributed Practice

While massed practice (performing all agility drills in one block) may result in the greatest acute learning, chronic learning is facilitated when agility drills are distributed throughout the session. Therefore, session and periodized programs need to take this into consideration.

Structuring the Agility Development Plan

The agility development plan should fit into a long-term plan of agility development. First, a base of simple, closed-movement skills should be built, and then developed into more complex open skills. Both short-term and long-term goals need to be set, with the aim of developing efficient and effective movement skills. Each session should have a specific goal and activities that contribute to that specific goal. Drills must be carefully thought out, and not just thrown together. Because technical correctness is crucial, the focus should be on quality not quantity.

The use of appropriate feedback cues can assist in the correct performance of the drills. Care should be taken to ensure that: the athlete develops basic movement patterns, progresses from simple-to-complex skills, and progresses from closed-to-open skills.

The session

The relative time spent on each section will vary with the athlete's experience. Beginner athletes will spend the greatest time on basic mechanics, while experienced athletes will spend more time on movement drills.

Warm-up

This phase should involve general temperature raising and dynamic flexibility-and-mobility activities. Technical drills should be used whenever possible.

Innervation

The neural pathways should be stimulated by the use of fast-feet drills, such as ladder work.

Mechanics

Predominantly closed movements should be performed until the basic mechanics have been developed.

Movement drills

The athlete should progress from closed to open movements. Resisted and assisted movements can be utilized in these practices.

Session Organization

The basic rules of periodization apply to agility session design. The program should be designed with consideration for phase, frequency, volume, rest, intensity, and progression.

Phase

The particular phase of the season (in-season, off-season, etc.) may impact the time and energy available for agility work. The athlete will have less time to work on the agility in-season, so it may be necessary to incorporate agility training into drills or conditioning. Also, the athlete will not be able to make the same gains in-season, as out of season. As a rule, more time will exist to focus on agility during the off-season or pre-season phases.

Frequency

Agility sessions should take place about two times a week in the preseason and off-season, and once a week during the season. Time is the biggest factor concerning frequency.

Volume

Volume refers to the number of times the drill or foot contacts are performed. It is better to keep the volume low and focus on doing the drill correctly. Racing through the drill more times will not develop the correct motor paths needed to reproduce the movement during game time.

Rest

Rest refers to the time between repetitions, sets, and workouts. Do not try to run the athletes until they get sick.

What energy system does the sport require? The agility workout should be tailored to develop this energy system. Some coaches call this metabolic training, while others call it sport-specific training. Whatever the terminology, the agility training must meet the demands of the sport. Just as in lifting, it is possible to overtrain athletes in the conditioning part of the workout.

Intensity

When athletes are first learning the movement patterns, it may be necessary to have them walk through the movements. As they become more comfortable with the patterns involved, the speed of the movements should be increased or made more random. Some coaches have the athlete verbally say the pattern (e.g., "left foot in/ right foot out"). Experience has shown that this practice helps the athlete learn the pattern faster and focus on the movement. In time, the athlete does not have to say it and the pattern becomes automatic.

Program Design

Each session should be designed with a specific goal in mind. Will it focus on balance, reaction, acceleration/deceleration, or body-movement control? Will the drills be open or closed, whole body or part? Remember, each session should have a specific purpose and goal. Proper layout will help achieve this objective.

Agility Drills Set in a Wrestling Room

One particularly appropriate place to conduct agility workouts is the wrestling room, a location that provides a safe surface, a controlled environment (where the athletes can easily be monitored), and an area where weather is not an issue. Diagram 9-1 illustrates a sample layout for conducting agility drills in a wrestling room. Such a developmental session should emphasize agility in all directions, reaction time, and the elimination of false steps. Enough recovery time between stations and repetitions should be allotted, so that the athletes can go 100% while they are doing the drills. The athletes should rotate in a clockwise direction. Keep in mind that the key factor is

Diagram 9-1: Sample agility drill workout layout in a wrestling room.

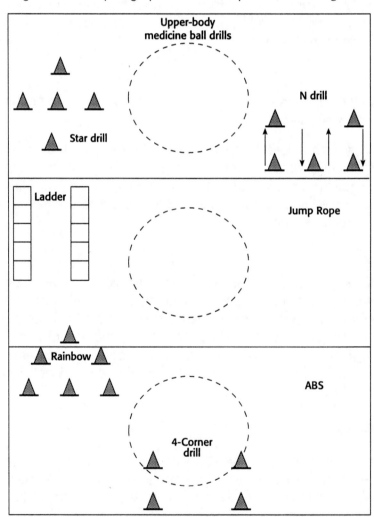

quality of motion, not how fast the athlete can go. Among the drills that can be included in such a workout are the following:

☐ *N drill*: The athlete runs forward and then puts their hand down at the top cone so they can make a 180-degree turn to the middle cone. With the hand down, while making a 180-degree turn, the athlete then goes to the second top cone. Repeating the turn to the last cone. Finally, the finish line becomes the start line for the second trip; this procedure allows the athlete to work both sides evenly.

☐ *Jump rope*: In the jump-rope station, any number of patterns or drills can be used.

☐ *ABS*: Abdominal or core exercises should stress the whole midsection, not just one muscle.

☐ *Four-corner drill*: The athlete starts at the bottom left corner, running forward to the top cone, performs a carioca across the top, backpedals to the bottom cone, and finishes with a shuffle to the bottom left cone. The drill should be performed in both directions by starting at the bottom left and bottom right cones.

☐ *Rainbow drill*: Starting at the bottom middle cone, the athlete shuffles to the left cone, touches it with their hand and shuffles back to the center cone. Next, the athlete runs to the left 45-degree cone, touches it, and shuffles back to the center cone. The athlete runs to the top cone, touches it, and backpedals to the center cone. Next, the athlete runs to the right 45-degree cone, touches it, and backpedals to the center cone. The athlete then shuffles to the right cone, touches it, and shuffles back. One possible variation of the drill can involve using a tennis ball. The coach stands at the top of the rainbow with a tennis ball, and rolls it to the cone they want the athlete to touch. The athlete picks up the ball and tosses it back. Another option is to have the coach number the cones, and call out the number of the cone they want the athlete to touch. This variation will make it more of a reaction drill.

☐ *Ladders*: See patterns

☐ *Star drill*: The athlete starts at the bottom of the star and runs to the center cone. The coach points which direction the athlete should go. If it is to the side, the athlete should open the hips trying not to cross the legs so they do not get tripped up. On the bottom cones, the athlete can either backpedal or open the hips at 180-degrees and run. The coach should be looking for false steps and slow reaction time.

☐ *Upper body medicine ball drills*: These developmental activities can be core-stability drills or reaction drills.

CHAPTER 10

Sample Power, Agility Speed Program

Patrick McHenry, MA, CSCS

Tables 10-1 and 10-2 provide examples of how to design workouts for different level athletes, while still achieving the same goal. The beginning group is designed so that the whole group does the drills together, while the intermediate/advanced workout is broken into smaller groups so the athletes involved in this workout can perform a more concentrated training session. Rest times, specific drills, and number of reps will be dependent upon the particular season the athlete is in (e.g., pre-season, off-season, or in-season).

Diagram 10-1 illustrates a template for a sample power, agility, and speed workout that is set up for a 2 or 4-day workout. The workout is designed so that the coach can plug in their own drills or use the sample drills. Two days are used to work on agility/speed, and two days are allotted for balance/coordination work. Laying the drills out helps to ensure that the focus of the workout is maintained.

Table 10-1. Sample power/agility/speed workout for beginners.

	Monday	**Tuesday**	**Wednesday**	**Thursday**
Agility	Ladder patterns 1-3		Ladder patterns 1-3	
Speed	Flag tag		Flag tag	
Balance		Beam walk		Beam walk
Coordination		Tennis-ball drills		Tennis-ball drills
Agility	Jump rope a-f		Jump rope a-f	
Speed	Hurdle 1-4		Hurdle 1-4	
Balance		Crazy ball		Crazy ball
Coordination		Octagon		Octagon
Agility	Cone drill W		Cone drill W	
Speed	Get up and go		Get up and go	
Balance		Swiss ball		Swiss ball
Coordination		3-joint med ball drills		3-joint med ball drills

Table 10-2. Sample power/agility/speed workout for intermediate-to-advanced athletes.

Monday/Wednesday	**Agility**
Group	Stations
A	Jumps in place (over cone/Hurdle)
B	Lateral jumps (ski in place)
C	Ladder patterns 1-3
D	Reaction ball drops
E	Jump rope patterns a-d
F	Cones (star)
G	Hurdle patterns 1-3
H	4-Point hand tag
Tuesday/Thursday	**Plyometric**
Group	Stations
A	Wall touches
B	Box drills (quick-feet patterns)
C	Chest press
D	Explosion throw
E	Box jump patterns 1-3
F	Roller ball
G	Frog hops
H	Tuck jumps

Diagram 10-1. An example of a template for a sample power, agility, and speed workout.

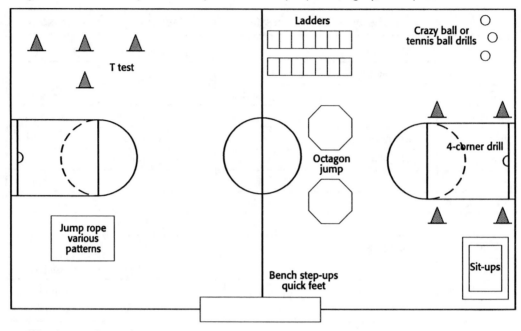

Agility/Speed Work

☐ *Ladder patterns*: See patterns

☐ *Flag-tag drill*: Set up a box, any size will work (e.g., 5'x5'), in which the athletes will have to stay. Each team gets a set of flag football flags and starts on the opposite side of the box. They have to get the other team's flags without having their own pulled. If an athlete loses a flag, they have to do pushups, and the other person has to move three feet away before the drill starts again.

☐ *Jump rope*: See patterns

☐ *Cone drill W*: Set up five cones in a "W" shape. The length should be 5-10 yards, and the width at least three yards. The athlete starts at the top and runs to the bottom cone. Going around that cone, the individual moves to the middle cone, goes around it, runs back to the bottom cone, and finishes at the top. The athlete repeats the drill from the side they ended on, training in both directions.

☐ *Get up and go drill*: Lying on his stomach, the athlete reacts to the coach's command, gets up, and sprints. This drill can also be done with the athlete starting by lying on their back.

Balance/Coordination Work

☐ *Beam walk*: Get a 2x4 or 4x4 and have the athlete walk across it. The individual can move forward, backward, or laterally. If several pieces of wood are available, the athlete can be made to go in a zigzag pattern.

☐ *Tennis-ball drill*: Have one person stand with their arms out and a tennis ball in each hand. The other person stands three feet away. As one tennis ball is dropped, the other person must grab the ball before it bounces twice. Another variation of the drill is to have the athlete with the tennis balls stand behind, while the other person sits. The balls are then rolled or bounced, so the athlete who is sitting has to get up and grab the ball.

☐ *Crazy-ball drill*: The athlete bounces an eight-sided ball to his partner, and both individuals have to react to it.

☐ *Octagon drill*: The octagon can be made out of PVC pipe and 45-degree joints, or the design can simply be taped on the floor. The athlete jumps into and out of the octagon in either a clock-wise, or counter-clockwise pattern. The athlete keeps the body pointed in one direction through the whole drill. This positioning causes the athlete to jump in different directions. This drill can be performed using one foot or two.

☐ *Swiss-ball drill*: Any drill on the swiss ball.

☐ *Three-joint medicine ball drill*: The athlete places the medicine ball on the ground between their hands, while they get into a three-point stance (often referred to as a football lineman's stance). The athlete explodes, using the legs, and throws the medicine ball against the wall. The athlete should be at least 15-20 yards from wall. The athlete is trying to work on the extension of the ankle, knee, and hip.

CHAPTER 11

Resistance Training in the Classroom

Patrick McHenry, MA, CSCS

Student Evaluation and Grading Criteria

The grading of student coursework in the high school, weight-training curriculum depends on the following key elements: state requirements, school policies, instructor philosophy, and objectivity.

The course objectives are the main criteria on which any evaluation process should be based. As such, these objectives provide the instructor with a tool to assist in evaluating the student's progress and acquisition of knowledge. The tools used to evaluate students will depend on the facilities and equipment available. An attempt should also be made to measure the student's understanding of all the skills to be learned. Strength gains and/or the amount that a student lifts should be secondary in evaluation. The following discussion focuses on the possible elements that can be included in the grading of a weight training class (psychomotor skills, cognitive skills, affective domain, class attendance, improvement/performance, and dress). It is designed to serve as a guideline that can be modified as appropriate.

Psychomotor Skills

Psychomotor skills offer a very important tool for evaluating the application of information learned in the classroom. In a testing situation, for example, the student may be asked to perform a specific exercise, using correct form. In addition, the student may be required to explain the technique, muscles used, prime movers, spotting technique, and breathing for that exercise. The student should also be able to evaluate correct and incorrect exercise techniques performed by other students. For students to safely and enjoyably participate in resistance training, they must learn the correct exercise technique. In learning correct exercise technique, students must actively take part in the execution of each exercise. Grading their psychomotor skills can be done formally (choosing one day to evaluate each student while they perform a specific exercise) or informally (evaluating students while they perform their workout).

Cognitive Skills

With regard to incorporating cognitive skills into the grading process, the instructor tries to ascertain whether the student has gained the essential knowledge pertinent to weight training. The main tool used to measure this factor is a written test. All students should be tested on their knowledge with regard to exercise technique, spotting, safety, program organization, and implementation. The student may be asked to explain the actions of the exercise techniques, identification of the muscle groups used, and appropriate exercises to develop specific muscle groups. Students may also be asked to make a 3-day diet analysis, design a sport-specific workout, or design a power/agility/speed workout. Any questions asked must be based on information provided in class and pertain to the type of equipment used during the course.

Table 11-1. Cognitive testing options.

Short answer essay	Positive Negative	Shows in-depth knowledge, integrating reading/writing Takes time to grade
Scan Tron	Positive Negative	Easy to take/ grade Does not show in-depth knowledge
Fill in Blank	Positive Negative	Easy grading/less time Allows for guessing. Does not show in-depth knowledge
Oral	Positive Negative	Shows in-depth knowledge Time consuming

With regard to grading, the number of points awarded for each evaluative factor is left up to the instructor. The number one factor that might change is attendance, depending on the number of class meetings held. How the instructor grades and the number of points given in each area depend on the instructor's philosophy and school policy. Table 11-1 provides an overview listing of possible cognitive options.

Affective Domain

Affective domain is related to a person's values, attitudes, interests, efforts, and social interactions. Objective areas for grading effort could be repetitions and sets (for example, did the students perform all of them), are the students using more weight on heavy days and less weight on light days, and are the students spotting or talking during the workout? While these attributes are difficult to measure, they are learned, and therefore can be subjectively evaluated by the instructor.

Class Attendance

As in any class, where the main objective is the attainment of skill in an activity, it is necessary that the student be present in class. If a student is injured, alternate reading assignments can be assigned to enable the student to earn class points. Articles or informational packets allow students to develop their affective domain while they attend class. The school may have a standard policy with regard to the number of absences permitted before the student's grade is affected.

Improvement/Performance

Another factor that can be utilized in the grading process is to test the student on improvement and/or performance. One possible problem with testing is if a student is graded on improvement, they may purposely not perform well on the initial test. During the second test, the student will then perform their best, thereby showing a great improvement from the first test.

Another potential problem with testing involves the disparities that can arise with evaluating an individual's performance. For example, students who already excel in strength development will show smaller increases in performance than the untrained.

A different testing method that can be used is a percentile or performance-ranking scale. Both of these tests do not consider increases in performance, but only absolute performance. Regardless, whether students are graded on improvement or performance, this measure should only count as a small percentage (5-10%) of the individual's overall grade.

Recognition for Outstanding Performance

To encourage hard work and recognize those students who excel, a record board or performance contest can be developed. While this instrument does not have to be part of a student's grade, it does provide a forum for the students to showcase their talents and get recognized for their efforts.

A record board should include both lifting (weight lifted, percent of body weight lifted, and body weight lifts) and running student performances, so all students, no matter how big or small, have a chance at success. After choosing the lifts and running tests, the board should be set up by weight class and grade.

Dress

Proper attire (shorts, shirt, and shoes) should be required in a resistance-training class. This requirement primarily is for safety and personal-hygiene reasons. Working out in everyday school clothes should not be allowed. Any clothing that is deemed inappropriate by the instructor should result in the loss of points in the student's grading scheme.

Weighted Scale

Once all the tests have been conducted, and points available have been determined, the instructor may want to incorporate a weighted scale. The weighted scale serves to put more emphasis (points) on the areas of the class that are most important. Points given in the class are multiplied by the weighted factor to provide total points. For example, social interaction may have a 25-point scale, with a weighted value of (1). On the other hand, exercise technique may have a 108-point scale, and a weighted factor of (3). Table 11-2 provides a sample grading matrix that employs a weighted scale.

Conversion Chart for the Grading Matrix

Once the instructor has reviewed the student's performance in detail, the scoring will normally need to be converted to a more commonly used grading scale. Common letter grades can then be derived. In this regard, Table 11-3 illustrates an example of a conversion chart that can be used to convert points earned to letter grades. As such, the instructor is able to incorporate all aspects contributing both to student learning of the content and to the student's performance in the training facility, in a fair and comprehensive manner.

Teacher Evaluation of Exercise Technique

On predetermined days, the students should be evaluated on exercise technique or spotting technique. Tables 11-4 and 11-5 illustrate sample forms that can be used by

Table 11-2. Sample grading matrix.

Area	Item	Points	Weighted Scale	Total Points	Percentage of Grade
Psychomotor	Exercise Technique	108	3	324	
	Spotting Technique	61	3	183	
Subtotal				507	33%
Cognitive	Quiz	50	1	50	
	Work out design	100	1	100	
	Quiz	50	1	50	
	Test-Final	100	3	100	
Subtotal				500	33%
Affective	Leadership	25	1	25	
	Attitude	25	1	25	
	Sportsmanship	25	1	25	
	Participation	25	1	25	
	Social Interaction	25	1	25	
Subtotal				125	8%
Attendance/Dress	Attendance	100	2	200	
	Dress	100	2	200	
Subtotal				400	25%
Total points				1532	

the instructor when evaluating exercise or spotting technique. When using these forms, the instructor should circle either the 0 or the 1, and total the 1's for that exercise. Table 11-6 provides a summary of the maximum points that may be scored for both the exercise technique and spotting activities of the student.

Teacher Evaluation of Student-Designed Workout

One optional assignment is to have the students design a resistance-training program. The teacher then evaluates the student's workout design. Table 11-7 provides a sample form that can be used to evaluate a student-designed program. For each of the ten categories listed in Table 11-7, the instructor gives the student a rating of 1 to 10 points and records that number in the points column.

Table 11-3. Sample conversion chart for grading.

Total Points	Percentage	Letter Grade
1501-1532	98-100	A+
1455-1500	95-97	A
1424-1454	93-94	A-
1378-1423	90-92	B+
1332-1377	87-89	B
1302-1331	85-86	B-
1256-1301	82-84	C+
1210-1255	79-81	C
1179-1209	77-78	C-
1149-1178	75-76	D+
1103-1148	72-74	D
1072-1102	70-71	D-
< or = 1071	< 70	F

Rating Categories

The following descriptions can be employed in observing and rating each factor included in Table 11-7:

- Goals: Does the program have a proper goal(s)? Muscular strength, muscular endurance, decreased body fat, increased lean body mass, and improved physique?
- Programs may include: total body, split workout, bodybuilding, Olympic lifting, and circuit training.
- Exercise selection: Are the selected exercises appropriate for the goals?
- Order of exercises: Are the exercises performed in the proper order? Explosive to non-explosive, core to assistant, large to small muscle groups, and multi-joint to single joint?
- Frequency: Does a minimum of 24 hours exist between workouts and 48 hours between exercising the same body parts?
- Intensity: Is the percentage of 1RM appropriate for the repetitions selected?
- Repetitions: Are the repetitions appropriate for the goals? Hypertrophy 8-20, strength 5-8, and power 3-5?

- Number of sets: 3 to 6 for core exercises and 2 to 3 for assistant exercises?
- Recovery periods: Is the recovery appropriate based on the program goals? 4-5 minutes for power, 2-3 minutes for strength, 1 1/2 minutes to 30 seconds for hypertrophy?
- Program progression: Does the program progress safely and properly?

Table 11-4. Sample form for evaluating exercise technique.

Evaluation of Exercise Technique	
Exercise:	
Date:	
Start:	
Grip position	0-1
Body position	0-1
Action-Negative:	
Breathing	0-1
Body position 0-1	
Bar movement	0-1
Bar speed	0-1
Action-Positive:	
Breathing	0-1
Body position 0-1	
Bar movement	0-1
Bar speed	0-1
Rack:	Y-N
Bar on rack	0-1
"Ok" given	0-1

Table 11-5. Sample form for evaluating spotting technique.

Evaluation of Spotting Technique

Exercise:

Date:

Start:

Grip position	0-1
Body position	0-1
Preparation for liftoff	0-1

Action-Negative:

Eyes on bar	0-1
Supervision of bar movement	0-1

Action-Positive:

Eyes on bar	0-1
Supervision of bar movement	0-1

Rack: Y-N

Grip position	0-1
Bar level	0-1
Placement on rack	0-1

Teacher Evaluation of a Student's Daily Performance

Another method of evaluating students is to give each student 10 points a day. If the student performs all the lifts and spots correctly, then they keep all 10 points. If they do not finish all their repetitions or miss on spotting, then the student loses points. Table 11-8 presents a sample form that can be used by the instructor to evaluate a student's lifting and spotting efforts.

Table 11-6. Summary of possible maximum points for exercise technique and spotting.

Exercise	Points	Spotting	Points
Squat	12 (rack)	Squat	10 (rack)
Bench Press	12 (rack)	Bench Press	10 (rack)
Incline Bench Press	12 (rack)	Incline Bench Press	10 (rack)
Shoulder Press	12 (rack)	Shoulder Press	10 (rack)
Dumbbell Bench Press	10	Dumbbell Bench Press	7
Dumbbell Incline Press	10	Dumbbell Incline Press	7
Bicep Curl	10		
Tricep Extension	10		
Lat Pull Down	10		
Bentover Row	10		

Table 11-7. Sample form for evaluating a student-designed program.

Student: Period:

Item	Points
Established goals	
Program selection	
Exercise selection	
Exercise order	
Training frequency	
Training intensities	
Number of repetitions	
Number of sets	
Recovery periods	
Program progression	
Total points (100 maximum)	

Table 11-8. Sample form for evaluating a student's daily performance.

Student: Period:

LIFT	Points for repetitions/sets		Points for spotting	
	Possible	Earned	Possible	Earned
Bench	1		1	
Squat	1		1	
Clean	1		1	
Incline	1		1	
Abs	1		1	
TOTAL	5		5	

Class Schedules

The format of each daily lesson plan should be structured in the following manner:

- Lecture, demonstration, question, and answer
- Workout
- Exercise technique (if assigned)
- Handouts and assignments

Lecture, Demonstration, Question-and-Answer Period

During this time, the instructor presents new information, demonstrates exercise techniques, and answers questions from the students on their reading assignment or handouts, previous lessons, or other pertinent information. During the lecture, the instructor presents the specific-content information outlined in the lesson plan for that class. Other faculty or non-faculty speakers may be brought in to supplement the basic lesson presentation on selected topics. During the demonstration and critique phase of the class, the instructor may choose to invite a student to perform a specified exercise, and then provide an objective critique of that student's performance with pointers.

Workout Period

Students perform the class workout, which will include a warm-up, stretching, training, and, in some instances, further demonstration. During the practical work, all students should attempt to perform the exercise previously demonstrated. This method allows instant feedback from the demonstration. This technique also provides the instructor with some time to observe the students.

Exercise Technique Period

The exercise technique period is designed to provide the student with the opportunity to demonstrate correct exercise preparation, technique, and communication with the spotter. Only one exercise should be evaluated during each class period. If the athlete sees the lift performed correctly, and is talked through doing the exercise properly, he will learn it faster.

Handouts and Assignments

At the conclusion of the class, reading assignments may be made, or handouts may be distributed. These handouts may either be from this manual or from other sources developed to meet the needs of the class in each situation.

APPENDIX

NSCA Strength and Conditioning Standards and Guidelines

Preface

The Strength & Conditioning profession is at a crossroads. It involves the combined competencies of sport/exercise science, administration, management, teaching and coaching. Its practitioners must also comply with various laws and regulations while responding to instances of potential injury, and related claims and suits. This creates remarkable challenges, and requires substantial experience, expertise and other resources to effectively address them—especially in multi-sport (e.g., collegiate and scholastic) settings.

Ample resources are available in some of these settings. In many others, however, they are not. Budgets, equipment, facilities and staff are often limited (or lacking altogether), with a resulting mismatch between the athletes' demand for safe and effective programs and services, and the institution's provision of them. It is important for Strength & Conditioning practitioners and their employers to understand that this standard of care is a shared duty; the institution and individual are thus jointly responsible for fulfilling it. Collectively, these issues are the driving forces behind this project.

The purpose of the *NSCA Strength & Conditioning Professional Standards & Guidelines* project is to help identify areas of liability exposure, increase safety and decrease the likelihood of injuries that might lead to legal claims and suits, and ultimately improve the standard of care being provided. This document is intended to be neither rigid nor static. On the contrary, the need for discretion and insight is a fundamental theme throughout; and the information presented here will be revised periodically as the profession continues to evolve. It is hoped that Strength & Conditioning practitioners and the institutions employing them will mutually benefit from applying this information, and in turn significantly enhance the quality of services and programs offered to their athletes.

Notice

This document is intended to provide relevant practice parameters for Strength & Conditioning professionals to utilize when carrying out their responsibilities in providing services to athletes or other participants. The standards and guidelines presented here are based on published scientific studies, pertinent statements from other associations, analysis of claims and litigation, and a consensus of expert views. However, this information is not a substitute for individualized judgment or independent professional advice.

Neither the NSCA nor the contributors to this project assume any duty owed to third parties by those reading, interpreting or implementing this information. When rendering services to third parties, these standards and guidelines cannot be adopted for use with all participants without exercising independent judgment and decision-making based on the Strength & Conditioning professional's individual training, education and experience. Furthermore, Strength & Conditioning practitioners must stay abreast of new developments in the profession so that these standards and guidelines may evolve to meet particular service needs.

Neither the NSCA nor the contributors to this project, by reason of authorship or publication of this document, shall be deemed to be engaged in practice of any branch of professional discipline (e.g., medicine, physical therapy, law) reserved for those licensed under state law. Strength & Conditioning practitioners utilizing this information are encouraged to seek and obtain such advice, if needed or desired, from those licensed professionals.

1. PREPARTICIPATION SCREENING & CLEARANCE

Standard 1.1 Strength & Conditioning professionals must require athletes to undergo health care provider screening and clearance prior to participation, in accordance with instructions specified by the *AAFP-AAP-AMSSM-AOSSM-AOASM Preparticipation Physical Evaluation Task Force*, the AHA & ACSM, as well as relevant governing bodies and/or their constituent members (e.g., the NCAA for collegiate athletes; state legislatures, or individual state high school athletic associations/districts for scholastic athletes). In recreational activity programs, Strength & Conditioning professionals must require participants to undergo preparticipation screening and clearance in accordance with AHA & ACSM recommendations. For children, the clearance decision must include a determination or certification than the child has reached a level of maturity allowing participation in such activities as addressed in the "Participation in Strength & Conditioning Activities by Children" standards statement (refer to item 8).

Guideline 1.1 Strength & Conditioning professionals should cooperate with a training participant's health care providers at all times, and provide service in the participant's best interest according to instructions specified by such providers.

2. PERSONNEL QUALIFICATIONS

Guideline 2.1 The Strength & Conditioning practitioner should acquire a bachelor's or master's degree from a regionally accredited college or university (verification by transcript or degree copy) in one or more of the topics comprising the "Scientific Foundations" domain identified in the *Certified Strength & Conditioning Specialist* (CSCS)® *Examination Content Description*, or in a relevant subject. An ongoing effort should also be made to acquire knowledge and skill in the other content areas.

Guideline 2.2 The Strength & Conditioning practitioner should achieve and maintain the CSCS® credential; and fulfill the continuing education program requirements of the NSCA CERTIFICATION COMMISSION. Depending on the practitioner's scope of activities, responsibilities, and knowledge requirements, relevant certifications offered by other governing bodies may also be appropriate.

Guideline 2.3 The productivity of a Strength & Conditioning staff, as well as learning and skill development of individual members, should be enhanced by aligning a performance team comprised of qualified practitioners with interdependent expertise and shared leadership roles. Once the team is assembled, respective activities and responsibilities from the "Practical/Applied" domain identified in the *Certified Strength & Conditioning Specialist* (CSCS)® *Examination Content Description*—as well as appropriate liaison assignments—should be delegated according to each member's particular "Scientific Foundations" expertise.

3. PROGRAM SUPERVISION & INSTRUCTION

Standard 3.1 Strength & Conditioning programs must provide adequate and appropriate supervision with well-qualified and trained personnel, especially during peak usage times. In order to ensure maximum health, safety, and instruction, Strength & Conditioning professionals must be present during Strength & Conditioning activities; have a clear view of the entire facility (or at least the zone being supervised by each practitioner) and the athletes in it; be physically close enough to the athletes under their care to be able to see and clearly communicate with them; and have quick access to those in need of spotting or assistance.

Standard 3.2 In conjunction with appropriate safety equipment (e.g. power racks), attentive spotting must be provided for athletes performing activities where free weights are supported on the trunk or moved over the head/face (refer to Earle & Baechle [Chapter 17, pp. 343-389] in *Essentials Of Strength Training & Conditioning*).

Guideline 3.1 Strength & Conditioning activities should be planned—and the requisite number of qualified staff (refer to item 2) should be available—such that recommended guidelines for minimum average floor space allowance per athlete (100 ft2), professional-to-athlete ratios (1:10 junior high school, 1:15 high school,

1:20 college), and number of athletes per barbell or training station (=3) are achieved during peak usage times. Younger participants, novices or special populations engaged in such Strength & Conditioning activities should be provided with greater supervision (refer to item 8). Strength & Conditioning practitioners and their employers should work together toward a long-term goal of matching the professional-to-athlete ratio in the Strength & Conditioning facility to each sport's respective coach-to-athlete ratio.

4. FACILITY & EQUIPMENT SET-UP, INSPECTION, MAINTENANCE, REPAIR & SIGNAGE

Standard 4.1 Exercise devices, machines and equipment—including free weights—must be assembled, set up and placed in activity areas in full accordance with manufacturer's instructions, tolerances and recommendations; and with accompanying safety signage, instruction placards, notices and warnings posted or placed according to ASTM standards so as to be noticed by users prior to use. In the absence of such information, professionals must complete these tasks in accordance with authoritative information available from other sources.

Standard 4.2 Prior to being put into service, exercise devices, machines or free weights must be thoroughly inspected and tested by Strength & Conditioning professionals to ensure that they are working and performing properly, and as intended by the manufacturer.

Standard 4.3 Exercise machines, equipment and free weights must be inspected and maintained at intervals specified by manufacturers. In the absence of such specifications, these items must be regularly inspected and maintained according to the Strength & Conditioning practitioner's professional judgment.

Standard 4.4 Exercise devices, machines, equipment and free weights which are in need of repair, as determined by regular inspection or as reported by users, must be immediately removed from service and locked "out of use" until serviced and repaired; and be re-inspected and tested to ensure that they are working and performing properly before being returned to service. If such devices are involved in incidents of injury, legal advisors or risk managers must be consulted for advice prior to service/repair or destruction.

Guideline 4.1 Strength & Conditioning professionals and their employers should ensure that facilities are appropriate for Strength & Conditioning activities. Factors to be reviewed and approved prior to activity include, but are not limited to, floor surfaces, lighting, room temperature and air exchanges (refer to Greenwood [Chapter 24, pp. 549-566] in *Essentials Of Strength Training & Conditioning*).

Guideline 4.2 Manufacturer provided user's manuals, warranties and operating guides should be preserved and followed (refer to item 6).

Guideline 4.3 All equipment, including free weights, should be cleaned and/or disinfected regularly as deemed necessary by staff. Users should be encouraged to wipe down skin-contact surfaces after each use.

5. EMERGENCY PLANNING & RESPONSE

Standard 5.1 Strength & Conditioning professionals must be trained and certified in current guidelines for cardiopulmonary resuscitation (CPR) established by AHA/ILCOR; as well as universal precautions for preventing disease transmission established by the CDC and OSHA. First Aid training/certification is also necessary if sportsmedicine personnel (e.g., MD or ATC) are not immediately available during Strength & Conditioning activities. New staff engaged in Strength & Conditioning activities should comply with this standard within six (6) months of employment.

Standard 5.2 Strength & Conditioning professionals must develop a written, venue-specific emergency response plan to deal with injuries and reasonably foreseeable untoward events within each facility. The plan must be posted at strategic areas within each facility, and practiced and rehearsed at least quarterly. The emergency response plan must be initially evaluated (e.g., by facility risk managers, legal advisors, medical providers and/or off-premise emergency response agencies) and modified as necessary at regular intervals. As part of the plan, a readily accessible and working telephone must be immediately available to summon on-premise and/or off-premise emergency response resources.

Guideline 5.1 The components of a written and posted emergency response plan should include: planned access to a physician and/or emergency medical facility when warranted, including a plan for communication and transportation between the venue and the medical facility; appropriate and necessary emergency care equipment on-site that is quickly accessible; and a thorough understanding of the personnel and procedures associated with the plan by all individuals.

6. RECORDS & RECORD KEEPING

Guideline 6.1 In conjunction with written policies and procedures, Strength & Conditioning professionals should develop and maintain various records including: manufacturer provided user's manuals, warranties and operating guides; equipment selection, purchase, installation, set-up, inspection, maintenance and repair records; personnel credentials; professional standards and guidelines; safety policies and procedures, including a written emergency response plan (refer to item 5); training logs, progress entries and/or activity instruction/supervision notes; injury/incident reports, preparticipation medical clearance, and return to participation clearance documents. In settings where participants are not otherwise required to sign protective legal documents (e.g., informed consent, agreement to participate, waiver) covering all athletically related activities, the Strength & Conditioning professional should have such legal documents prepared for athletes under his/her care. These records should be preserved and maintained for a period of time determined by professional legal advice and consultation.

7. EQUAL OPPORTUNITY & ACCESS

Standard 7.1 Strength & Conditioning professionals and their employers must provide facilities, training, programs, services and related opportunities in accordance with all laws, regulations and requirements mandating equal opportunity, access and non-discrimination. Such federal, state and possibly local laws and regulations apply to most organizations, institutions and professionals. Discrimination or unequal treatment based upon race, creed, national origin, sex, religion, age, handicap/disability or other such legal classifications is generally prohibited.

8. PARTICIPATION IN STRENGTH & CONDITIONING ACTIVITIES BY CHILDREN

Guideline 8.1 Children under seven (7) years of age should not be permitted to engage in Strength & Conditioning activities with free weights or exercise devices/machines in facilities designed for use by adults and adolescents, and should be denied access to such training areas. Other forms of Strength & Conditioning activities may be beneficial for such children, and should be recommended according to the practitioner's professional judgment, and with a greater degree of instruction and supervision than that supplied to adolescents and adults. Children participating in such activities should be cleared as specified in the NSCA's "Standard for Preparticipation Screening & Clearance" (refer to item 1).

Guideline 8.2 Children between seven (7) and fourteen (14) years of age who have reached a level of maturity allowing participation in specified Strength & Conditioning activities, as determined and certified by their medical care provider (or by the Strength & Conditioning professional acting in concert with a child's medical care provider), and after clearance for participation as specified in the NSCA's "Standard for Preparticipation Screening & Clearance" (refer to item 1), should be individually assessed by the Strength & Conditioning professional in conjunction with the child's parent(s)/guardian(s)/custodian(s) and health care provider(s) to determine if such children may engage in such activities in areas containing free weights and exercise devices/machines generally used by adults and older children. If so permitted, such activities should be developed and implemented according to the practitioner's professional judgment, in conjunction with the child's health care provider(s), and with a greater degree of instruction and supervision than that supplied to adolescents and adults.

Guideline 8.3 Children fourteen (14) years of age and older who, according to the Strength & Conditioning practitioner's professional judgment, have reached a level of maturity allowing them to engage in specified Strength & Conditioning activities (provided they have been cleared for participation as specified in the NSCA's "Standard for Preparticipation Screening & Clearance"; refer to item 1), may engage in such activities in areas containing free weights and exercise devices/machines generally used by adults, and with a greater degree of instruction and supervision than that supplied to adult populations while training.

9. SUPPLEMENTS, ERGOGENIC AIDS & DRUGS

Standard 9.1 Strength & Conditioning professionals must not prescribe, recommend or provide drugs, controlled substances or supplements that are illegal, prohibited, or harmful to athletes for any purpose including enhancing athletic performance, conditioning or physique. Only those substances that are lawful and have been scientifically proven to be beneficial—or at least not harmful—may be recommended or provided to athletes by Strength & Conditioning professionals.

NSCA Professional Standards & Guidelines Task Force

Mike Brass, MS, CSCS
Assistant Athletic Director—Sports Performance
Georgia Southern University
P.O. Box 8082, Hanner Complex
Statesboro, GA 30460-1000

JoAnn Eickhoff-Shemek, PhD, FACSM
Associate Professor—School of Health, Physical Education & Recreation
University of Nebraska at Omaha
HPER 207, 60th & Dodge St.
Omaha, NE 68182-0216

Boyd Epley, MEd, CSCS
Assistant Athletic Director—Athletic Performance
University of Nebraska
100 West Stadium
Lincoln, NE 68588-0217

David Herbert, JD, Esq
Senior Partner
Herbert & Benson, Attorneys and Counselors at Law
4571 Stephen Circle N.W.
Canton, OH 44718-3629

Joe Owens, MS, CSCS,*D
Assistant Athletic Director–Strength & Conditioning
University of Dayton
300 College Park
Dayton, OH 45469-0001

David Pearson, PhD, CSCS,*D
Associate Professor–School of Physical Education
Ball State University
Human Performance Lab, PL 142
Muncie, IN 47306-1022

Steven Plisk, MS, CSCS • Chair
Director of Sports Conditioning
Yale University
P.O. Box 208216
New Haven, CT 06520-8216

Dan Wathen, MS, ATC, CSCS,*D, NSCA-CPT,*D
Athletic Training Coordinator
Youngstown State University
Stambaugh Stadium 1103
Youngstown, OH 44555-0001

Acknowledgments

The *NSCA Professional Standards & Guidelines Task Force* would like to thank the following individuals and organizations for their contribution to this project:

NSCA Certification Commission
Tom Baechle, EdD, CSCS,*D, NSCA-CPT,*D • Executive Director
Roger Earle, MA, CSCS,*D, NSCA-CPT,*D • Associate Executive Director

NSCA College Strength & Conditioning Professionals Special Interest Group
John Taylor, MS, CSCS,*D • Executive Council

NSCA Education Committee
Al Biancani, EdD, CSCS,*D
Helen Binkley, PhD, ATC, CSCS,*D
John Cissik, MS, CSCS
Jeff Fahrenbruch, MPT, CSCS,*D
Doug Kleiner, PhD, ATC, CSCS,*D • Chair
Mike Greenwood, PhD, CSCS,*D
Linda Grimm Lawyer, MS, CSCS
Patrick McHenry, MA, CSCS

Lisa Reed, MS, CSCS
Travis Triplett-McBride, PhD, CSCS
Kelly Williams, PhD, CSCS

NSCA National Office
Michael Barnes, MEd, CSCS • Director of Education
Keith Cinea,MA, CSCS • Educational Products Coordinator
Brian Newman, MS, CSCS • Senior Education Programs Coordinator

Reviewers
Dean Aresco, MA, CSCS
Anthony Auriemmo, MS, CSCS,*D
Thomas Battaglia, MS, CSCS
Michael Doscher, MS, CSCS
Allen Hedrick, MA, CSCS
William Klika III, CSCS
Dennis Kline, MS, CSCS
John McFarland, ATC/L, CSCS
Adam Miller, MA, CSCS
Ron Thomson, MA, CSCS
Russell Whitt, MEd, CSCS

Joint Commission on Sports Medicine & Science
American Academy of Family Physicians
American Academy of Pediatrics
American Chiropractic Association, Council on Sports Injuries & Physical Fitness
American College of Sports Medicine
American Kinesiotherapy Association
American Medical Society for Sports Medicine
American Optometric Association, Sports Vision Section
American Orthopedic Society for Sports Medicine
American Osteopathic Academy for Sports Medicine
Centers for Disease Control & Prevention
National Association for Sports & Physical Education
National Athletic Trainers' Association
National Collegiate Athletic Association
Physiatric Association of Spine, Sports & Occupational Rehabilitation
President's Council on Physical Fitness & Sports

As the worldwide authority on Strength & Conditioning, the National Strength & Conditioning Association supports and disseminates research-based knowledge and its practical application to improve athletic performance and fitness. Its goal is to unify members and facilitate a professional exchange of ideas in strength development as it relates to the improvement of athletic performance and fitness.

Since its inception in 1978, the NSCA has been working hard with well known industry experts to enhance, enlighten, and advance the field of Strength & Conditioning. The NSCA brings together a unique and diverse group of professionals from the sport science, athletic, and fitness industries. Its membership of over 19,000 professionals is comprised of Strength & Conditioning coaches, personal trainers, exercise physiologists, athletic trainers, researchers, educators, sport coaches, physical therapists, business owners, exercise instructors, fitness directors, and students training to enter the field. The NSCA provides its members with a wide variety of resources and opportunities designed to enhance their education and careers, including exceptional professional journals, cutting-edge conferences, scholarship and grant opportunities, educational texts and videos, and career services.

National Strength & Conditioning Association
1955 N. Union Blvd.
Colorado Springs, CO 80909
tel: 800 815-6826 or 719 632-6722   fax: 719 632-6367
e-mail: nsca@nsca-lift.org   http://www.nsca-lift.org/menu.asp

The NSCA Certification Commission offers two of the finest and only nationally accredited certification programs: the *Certified Strength & Conditioning Specialist* (CSCS)®; and the *NSCA Certified Personal Trainer* (NSCA-CPT)SM. These credentials have become the measure of excellence in the Strength & Conditioning profession.

NSCA Certification Commission
1640 L St., Suite G
Lincoln, NE 68508
tel: 888 746-CERT or 402 476-6669   fax: 402-476-7141
e-mail: commission@nsca-cc.org   http://www.nsca-cc.org/

REFERENCES

ACSM. (2000). Position statement: nutrition and athletic performance. *Medicine & Science in Sports & Exercise.* 32, 2130-2145.

Allerheiligen, B. & Rogers, R. (1995). Plyometrics program design. Strength and Conditioning Journal, 17(4), 26-31.

Baechle, T., & Earle, R. (Eds.). (2000). *Essentials of strength training and conditioning.* Champaign, IL: Human Kinetics.

Baechle, T. & Groves, B. (1972). *Weight training: Steps to success.* Champaign, IL: Leisure Press.

Baker, D., Wilson, G., & Carlyon, R. (1994). Periodization: The effect on strength of manipulating volume and intensity. *Journal of Strength and Conditioning Research.* 8, 235-242.

Benardot, D., Clarkson, P., Coleman, E., & Manore, M. (2001) Can vitamin supplements improve sports performance? *GSSI Sports Science Exchange Roundtable*, #45. 12(3).

Bobbert, M. (1990). Drop jumping as a training method for jumping ability. *Sports Medicine*, 9(1), 7-22.

Brooks, G., Fahey, T., & White, T. (1996). Exercise physiology: human bioenergetics and its application. Mountain View, CA: Mayfield Publishing Company.

Casa, D., Armstrong, L., Hillman, S., Montain, S., Reiff, R., Rich, B., Roberts, W., & Stone, J. (2000). National Athletic Trainers' Association position statement: fluid replacement for athletes. Journal of Athletics Training. 35, 212-224.

Cheuvront, S. (1999) The 'Zone' diet and athletic performance. *Sports Medicine.* 27, 213-28.

Chu, D. (1984). Plyometric Exercise. NSCA Journal, 5(6), 56-63.

Chu, D. (1998). Jumping into plyometrics. Champaign, IL: Human Kinetics.

Deutz B., Benardot, D., Martin, D., & Cody, M. (2000). Relationship between energy deficits and body composition in elite female gymnasts and runners. *Medicine & Science in Sports & Exercise.* 32, 659-668.

Fleck, S., & Kraemer, W. (1997). *Designing resistance training programs.* Champaign, IL: Human Kinetics.

Foran, Bill. (2001). *High-performance sports conditioning*. Champaign, IL: Human Kinetics.

Fox, E., Bowers, R., & Foss, M. (1989). The physiological basis of physical education and athletics. Dubuque, IA: Wm. C. Brown Publishers.

Gambetta, V. (1987). Principles of plyometric training. *Track Technique*, Fall, 1987.

Gatorade Sports Science Institute. (2002). 2002 GSSI guidelines on heat safety in football: Attacking heat-related death and illness in football players. [online]. http://www.gssiweb.com/reflib/refs/566/attackheatill.cfm?pid=38

Goldberg, A., Etlinger, J., Goldspink, L., & Jablecki, C. (1975). Mechanism of work-induced hypertrophy of skeletal muscle. *Medicine & Science in Sports & Exercise*. 7:248-261.

Hedrick, A. (2000). Dynamic flexibility training. *Strength and Conditioning Journal*, 22(5), 33-38.

Komi, P., & Bosco, C. (1978). Utilization of stored elastic energy in leg extensor muscles by men and women. Medicine and Science in Sport and Exercise, 10, 261-265.

Koziris, L. P., (1995). Varied multiple set resistance training program produces greater gain than single set program. *Medicine and Science in Sports and Exercise*. 27, S195.

Kramer, J., Stone, M.H., O'Bryant, H., Conley, M., Johnson, R., Nieman, D., Honeycutt, D., & Hoke, T. (1997). Effects of single vs. multiple sets of weight training: Impact of volume, intensity, and variation. *Journal of Strength and Conditioning Research*. 11, 143-147.

Kraemer, W. (1997) A series of studies: The physiological basis for strength training in American football: Fact over philosophy. *Journal of Strength and Conditioning Research*. 11, 31-142.

Lamb, D. (1995). Basic principles for improving sport performance. *GSSI Sports Science Exchange*, #55. 8(2).

Lord, P. & Campagna, P. (1997). Drop height selection and progression in a drop jump program. *Strength and Conditioning*, 19(6), 65-69.

Make the play. (1998). Lincoln: Husker Power.

Manore, M. & Thompson, J. (2000). Sports nutrition for health and performance. Champaign, IL: Human Kinetics.

McArdle, W., Katch, F., & Katch, V. (1999). *Sports & exercise nutrition*. Philadelphia: Lippincott Williams & Wilkins.

McFarlane, B. (1987). Warm-up pattern design. *NSCA Journal*, 9(4), 22-29.

O'Shea, Patrick. (2000). *Quantum Strength and Fitness II*, Corvallis, OR: Patrick's Books.

Radcliff, J. (1998). *High Powered Plyometrics*. Champaign, IL: Human Kinetics.

Radcliff, J. (Presenter). (2001). back to basics training: Plyometrics [Conference]. Spokane: NSCA.

Sale, D. (1988). Neural adaptation to resistance training. *Medicine & Science in Sports & Exercise*, 20, S135-S145.

Siff, M. & Verkhoshansky, Y. (2000). *Supertraining*. Denver: Supertraining.

Stone M. H., Plisk, S., Stone, M. E., Schilling, B., O'Bryant, H., Pierce, K. (1998). Athletic performance development: volume load - 1 set vs. multiple sets, training velocity and training variation. *Strength & Conditioning*, 20(6), 22–31.

Stowers, T., McMillan, J., Scala, D., Davis, V., Wilson, D., & Stone, M.H. (1983). The short-term effects of three different strength-power training methods. NSCA Journal, 5(3), 24-27.

Wathen, Dan. (1993). *Literature review: Explosive/plyometric exercise*. NSCA Journal, 15(3), 17-19.

Williams, M. (2002). Nutrition for health, fitness, & sport. Boston: McGraw-Hill.

Willoughby, D. (1993). The effects of mesocycle-length weight training programs involving periodization and partially equated volumes on upper and lower body strength. *Journal of Strength and Conditioning Research*. 7, 2-8.

EXCEPTIONAL DVDs ON STRENGTH AND CONDITIONING